LEAD
IS MALE?

*The issue of women
in leadership in the Church*

By
JACQUES MORE

JAROM BOOKS

Published by *Jarom Books*
London – UK

www.jarom.net

Printed and bound by
CPI Mackays, Chatham ME5 8TD

To my friend François-Luc
who foresaw the day there would
be more than one book

CONTENTS

PREFACE

There are few topics as sensitive on the emotional and spiritual fronts as that of the role of women in contrast to men. It is of all the potatoes one of the 'hottest' to handle. The emotional side can be visualised quite readily as sensitive but not always the spiritual. In his first letter to Timothy Paul mentions that one of the common teachings of demons, in particular deceiving spirits that try and influence a believer's faith, is that of forbidding to marry (1 Timothy 4:1-3). Relationships with the opposite sex and balance in their original intended roles are prime targets for the Devil and have been from the beginning.

The issue of men and women in Church leadership and related functions being so full of such emotional and spiritual considerations, it is sad but not surprising that sight has been lost on both 'sides' (of the theological divide) of clear admonition to love, forgive and be real brothers and sisters in Christ.

My own attempts to talk with writers on both 'sides' have been spurned in spite of stated desire to be otherwise in some of their own writings. Jesus, Paul, John all laid as much emphasis on how we behave towards one another as on doctrine. Indeed, Paul says if you know all but do not love you are nothing (1 Corinthians 13:2) and he made the excellent remark '**knowledge puffs up, but love edifies**' (1 Corinthians 8:1). Equally John recognized that if you did not love your brother, you may as well be hating God (1 John 4:20).

If you agree or disagree with me and this book, with due regard to whatever practical considerations (time and numbers of people), I hope to remain true to you in being willing to talk, out of genuine love for you.

My journey into this subject

After years of reading my Bible as a Christian I began to inquire as to the basis in Scripture for both the view that women should not be in leadership over men (nor teach them) and the basis for the opposite standpoint. I believed at the time that I was neutral and did not really have an opinion one way or the other. My concern was: what did the bible have to say about this?

I was aware from letters to the editor in *Renewal* magazine that articles on both sides of the proverbial fence had been produced previously. I contacted the magazine and was sent copies of all the relevant earlier articles which I proceeded to study with careful reference to the biblical data offered. In honesty what I felt then is that the argument for male leadership was expounded more out of the text than appeared to be the case for the opposite view: there was one or two points raised there which I felt were read into the Bible narrative.

Visiting my local Christian bookshop I noticed that *Leadership Is Male* by David Pawson published by Highland was for sale and I purchased a copy. David was the writer of the earlier read articles for male leadership. So I looked at this book with reference to my bible, and it was very much this teaching which I took on board as what seemed the most appropriate counsel which tied to the biblical data. On the whole I remained an advocate and supporter of this view for a number of years and recall even preaching on it once.

It was not until I had finished writing the manuscript for my first book that I began to read a number of other authors on the issue. I was not persuaded away from my main stand as such, but began to question the fact that if deception was a problem, why would Paul allow a woman to teach children and not apparently men (2 Timothy 1:5, Titus 2:3-4 contrasted with 1 Timothy 2:12), since children would be more vulnerable than grown ups in receiving teaching? I believe I first picked up this argument when reading Elaine Storkey's *What's Right With Feminism* SPCK. In itself this is an important argument towards a different understanding of 1 Timothy 2:12. The creation order however still remained both in 1 Timothy and in 1 Corinthians (e.g. 1 Corinthians 11:3) as a hook for retaining a male leadership position.

My turning point

My turning point, as it can rightly be called, because it was quite a sudden one, actually came when I read afresh what appears to be an unrelated passage of scripture: Mark 2.27: '**The Sabbath was made for man, and not man for the Sabbath.**' The context in which Jesus says this relates to the way the Sabbath rest command given by God was used as a means to impose extra guidelines never originally intended in the purpose for a day of rest. Jesus saying this highlighted for me the reason God made all creation in six days. It was only for an example of a day of rest to be had after six days work had been undertaken. Meditating on God's purpose in creating in this fashion (since He could have done it in four days or, seven minutes, etc.) made me think about why He made woman after man in the way He did. This made me look afresh at the clear direct and immediate context of this act of creation. If the Sabbath can be so misused beyond the general simple idea for cessation of work for 1 day after 6 of labour, how much more could this be true for the emotionally charged issue of the roles of the two genders?

So here I am as a 'convert' from 'male leadership' to a 'full role for women in leadership'. I explain in this book principles and passages in my own manner, as the foundation I presently hold for advocating that there is no biblical basis for preventing women to teach men or exercise leadership responsibility over them within certain guidelines.

The Title

I chose *Leadership is Male?* in part due to the history of my understanding of this topic. David Pawson's *Leadership is Male* is such a concise 'says it all' title and it's contents pretty much how I saw things for a time that just to add a question mark on the end sufficed very nicely (Thank you very much!). David is no stranger to doing this since his book *Once Saved, Always Saved?* is his effort in sharing the opposite view to author R.T.Kendall's earlier book *Once Saved, Always Saved*.

Note for the book

The New Testament of the bible was originally written in Koiné Greek. When Alexander the Great invaded the regions of the Middle East and North Africa, Greek became the language of commerce and general contacts between peoples. This was still the case by the time the Romans conquered these regions. It was a little later that Latin took over this function.

Due to the simplicity of reading, where Greek words are mentioned in this book the words are anglicised. So *andros* is the Genitive form of the word *anér*: the Greek word for 'man' or, 'husband'. You will note I have used an '*é*' (an accented 'e') in the basic word. This is in place of the Greek letter *eta* since Greek has '2' types of 'e'; the other being *epsilon* = 'e'. Similarly Greek has '2' types of 'o', for *omega* therefore the accented 'ò' will be used; the other being *omicron* = 'o'.

1

A FURTHER INTRODUCTION

The French Revolution gave France the motto 'Liberté, Egalité, Fraternité' – Liberty, equality, brotherhood: Quite an ideal but, "What about the sisters?"

Well, of course they are included in that, but it seems that when you look at the word 'brotherhood' and you are a legalist, immediately the word could be used to imply this is a 'male thing' and sisters are excluded.

Now, you may ask, what has this got to do with church leadership?

Well, it is that the authority for restricting women from equal roles as men is due to the bible. The bible is the ground upon which this is done. The very book which is scripture to Christians is one that should be seen to promote freedom, equality and brotherhood. But, it is due to its very contents which (apparently) omit the specific and clear mention of women in full blown leadership roles in the church which has caused the problem to a legalistic enquirer. Now, by legalistic I do not mean a dishonest or insincere investigator, but a person who would do the right thing based solely upon the words explicit within the Bible. Maybe legalistic is too strong a term for someone wishing to do the right thing, but it is a good one for use in connection with the enemy of all our souls, the Devil. For he will use whatever is available to him in the words of scripture to 'legally' bind and prevent freedom and release to men and women everywhere. This I believe is what he has done as regards to this issue.

Car electrics

So the issue lies in a few passages which have been looked at, studied, taken apart and discussed by a great many people before me. I will therefore look at these also. But, why should I be considered to have something new to offer?

This is a valid question. And I could answer this in a number of ways, but one immediately comes to my mind. Most of my working life has been as a car mechanic maintaining and fixing motor vehicles. One garage I worked at used to deal in Rovers. And in the time I was there it became apparent that I did not shy away from the electrical faults these were experiencing. The SD1 Rover being the main contender in those days (the early 1980s). A little reputation built up such that the Branch Manager, a previous mechanic himself, once came up to me and said: "Of course, after others have had a go and could not fix these electrical faults, you had a ready knowledge of what had not been tried . . .".

By this he implied that as I fixed these cars I went straight to the fault others had missed due to the knowledge of everything else tried which did not work. Nice try, but I held my peace.

What was not realised is that no such communication went on of this kind in general between the mechanics because by this time any one having possibly already looked at the problem would have been occupied elsewhere by the time it was given me to do. And one always started these jobs 'from scratch'. But, from a youth I've always had a love for Physics as a subject and a desire to understand how things work. So much so that a full appreciation and understanding of how electricity worked has meant that I often went back to basics when encountering an electrical problem. This was the main difference in my approach to fixing these things.

Plus, of course, that as a believer I would often ask the Lord's help ☺.

The Mathematician

Now scripture is such because it is inspired by the greatest Mathematician and Logical and Balanced Person alive: God Himself. And the Bible clearly says that He is light and in Him is no darkness at all (1 John 1:5). So my approach has been logical on the one hand, but because this Author is the living God I have not been alone. We are told plainly that if we seek wisdom we need only ask and He is ready to supply (James 1:5). And without the Holy Spirit I cannot claim any credit for the discoveries and truths now expanded in this book. I may have a mechanic's mind, but His use of the channel does not make me the Source of the wisdom in these pages.

So what are these passages that for a time persuaded me and still now hold so many in a belief that 'leadership is male'?

I will now share these in the next chapter and explain why these 'kept me' from believing for a full role for women in leadership. I aim to show why the explanations of advocates for 'equality' did not fit logically. I will call this the way things were or, *The Status Quo* Followed by *A Litany of Eisegesis*.

Then, there will be a going back to basics. A look at the very passages involved will reveal that why they could not mean one thing is because the translation itself is sometimes in question. Ah! Straightaway you may say, but how can we verify that what I say they mean is realistic? This is a very fair question.

Therefore I have included as much basic New Testament Greek grammar, research and appendices to help show the very things I am saying are valid. When I wanted to see if an electrical item on a car had a good connection to the negative side of the 12 volt battery, what we call 'the earth', I went back to basics. I used a jump lead. I tested that lead with a bulb or tester to see that itself the lead was good. Then after connecting it to the negative terminal of the battery I would then bypass the earth of the car body to the item in question and by this check I learned if that side of things was ok. And so on.

In other words just as with a hand torch the batteries inside are the source of the electrical power, one side of the battery connects to the body of the torch (it's earth) and the other side of the battery to one of the bulb connections. The switch being the main other link to the other bulb contact (normally then connecting the earth). All I was doing was by-passing the switch by connecting a cable to the earth side of the battery and the bulb. Not forgetting in my sharing this with you that with earlier cars the earth was the positive terminal and the process would be done via that end of things. The method of going back to basics is the essential.

Similarly here I will use basics to demonstrate why particular translations have not been working. And by this 'jump' or bypass, the many things that have side tracked us all for so long in the 'grand scheme of things' will be revealed and dealt with. Then we will have something that works and runs well as we re-start things with everything in a proper place.

2

THE STATUS QUO

Or, why the scriptures relevant, basically read,
point to male leadership.

This chapter is things as I saw it until 'turned'. It is a simple explanation of why all the arguments and views based on a cultural or, a particular historical setting did not work for me. All the attempts to view the passages in the light that today's culture and background do not hold the same application of those scriptures did not persuade me.

I have had no desire to write this book in a high brow intellectual quagmire which only the well read can appreciate. I wish this to be accessible to as many as have a love for the truth of the Word. Having said that, of course there needs be sufficient material to provide a firm foundation and back up the arguments I will make. This is provided for by the various sections relevant: The appendices in particular. But most should be able to understand what I am saying within the main chapters of the book. So, there will be no detailed pulling apart of the arguments by others as regards cultural or, historical reasoning. Except for the next chapter *A litany of Eisegesis* there is no such 'pulling apart'. Together with this chapter these two help to show why I kept to a view that 'leadership is male'. This is also the way things are for thousands of churches of many denominations worldwide. For these the prohibition comes primarily from three texts in the New Testament. These are within the chapters of 1 Corinthians 11, 1 Corinthians 14 and 1 Timothy 2. They are the three main passages which speak of these things and prevent these churches from permitting women in leadership. The reason made in these passages is based on two arguments. I would like then to concentrate in onward chapters on the two issues, Paul's two arguments, which are the 'sticking points': One at a time.

Two arguments

There are two simple arguments Paul makes for 'apparently' not permitting women to teach and which in turn exclude them from church leadership in contrast to the male gender. The first one involves the creation order and the second involves deception. This is best seen by his expansion upon probably the 'toughest' statement of all:

> I do not permit a woman to teach or to have authority over a man, but to be in silence. *1 Timothy 2:12*

These do appear as strong words, don't they?

Certainly, anyone with a love for God and believing in the inspiration of the Bible will be struck by this firm and apparently absolute statement. What other words could you use to say the same thing? This is why there are many sincere believers who practise male leadership.

What is even more striking is Paul's expansion and continuing words:

> For Adam was formed first, then Eve. *1 Timothy 2:13*

This is his first argument. Followed by,

> And Adam was not deceived, but the woman being deceived
> fell into transgression. *1 Timothy 2:14*

This is his second argument.

Now the creation order and the event of Eve's deception in the garden before sin and thus before 'the Fall' are in no way, shape or form, reasons to be side-tracked by beliefs in cultural or historical settings. They are concrete and solid arguments based on a time before culture and history played a part. Indeed before sin itself existed in man's experience.

Same arguments elsewhere

To also suggest that these arguments are part of an isolated thinking by Paul is also untrue. In another chapter to a separate letter, and that to a different church setting altogether – to the Corinthians – Paul uses these same arguments for a similar matter related to gender.

The creation order argument is seen by the following words:

> For man is not from woman, but woman from man. Nor
> was man created for the woman, but woman for the man.
> *1 Corinthians 11:8-9*

The deception argument I believe is also alluded to in Corinthians by the following remark:

> For this reason . . . because of the angels.
> *1 Corinthians 11:10*

Of course I need to unpack that particular set of words to show this reasoning and I do this later. By that I mean the deception argument is not immediately visible by that statement. It is an allusion to it.

Not a cultural foundation

So, as we can see above two separate passages pertaining to matters relating to gender show both the arguments of the creation order and deception as reasons or, foundations for these matters.

This is why no amount of twisting and turning explanations, involving culture or particular historical settings have ever satisfied me in the light of these two simple arguments by Paul.

My personal experience of deception and how the enemy works, my ensuing studies and learning on that topic, then helped me to see a way through the deception argument, but the creation order 'stuck': So that, my 'turning' came when that was firmly 'unstuck'. And I go into detail about this in chapter 11 entitled *The Creation Order & My Turning Point*.

Suffice to say I don't need to add much more to these two simple arguments by Paul at this stage to show why nothing I read persuaded me that the scripture which these passages are all a part of indicated anything other than male leadership. That is, until the context and thereby fuller hermeneutics came to light.

The three texts

In quoting 1 Timothy 2 above I have introduced for the first time one of 'the 3'. Here are the other two in order of appearance:

But I want you to know that the head of every man is Christ, the head of woman *is* man, and the head of Christ *is* God.

1 Corinthians 11:3

Let your women keep silent in the churches, for they are not permitted to speak; but *they are* to be submissive, as the law also says. And if they want to learn something, let them ask their own husbands at home; for it is shameful for women to speak in church. *1 Corinthians 14:34-35*

3

A LITANY OF EISEGESIS

Or, why authors 'for women' did not persuade me

———————

A litany is a list of prayers to be repeated: A series of petitions or requests to be made to the Lord in a church service. I use this word here as the name for a list of examples or, as I see ex-requests of bible texts used out of context to 'say' something. Passages used to declare or associated with the teaching of allowing a role for women in leadership. I hope to show with these passages that once I had read them and seen the context and the language used they were not 'saying' what was attributed to them. This is why I use the word eisegesis which is the arch-counterpart of exegesis. Good hermeneutics the study of the Bible in all relevant contexts produces sound exegesis. The alternative is eisegesis the reading of something into a passage instead of out of it.

Here follows some of the passages I have come across and as I endeavour to explain their context or language I trust you will see why they did not persuade me. I could not in reading the bible alongside these understandings honestly be persuaded that this was what the text was saying. This being so it is of value to share these and the thinking involved to help freedom to be realised from the nuances and misunderstandings they have been party to.

There is need however to be careful in that those who have shared these teachings need to be left unmentioned. Their motives and desires are not in question, nor their faith in God or the Bible. And any mention of their names brings into play, in a publicly read book, new readers access to these people and ministries in a manner which can lead to mistrust which may be unwarranted. The continuing use of these passages, in the manner I will explain, will suffice to show any degree in which trust can be gauged, but the mention of the name or ministry would go beyond the injunction to do to others what you would have them do to you (Matthew 7:12). So, I have chosen not to mention who wrote these and taught in this manner. If a name is mentioned, then the good teaching they do impart has the opportunity to be doubted. The believer is under the injunction to test all things and that action is to be continuously practised. This is true of what you are reading now. You should weigh it up. Any name calling in this setting (there is a place for it) can lead to putting a ministry in a box and lead to an excuse not to actively check out what one hears for oneself. But, we are told also to hold to the good. It is in holding the good produced by these writers that I do not mention their names (1 Thessalonians 5:21).

'Obey Sarah'

God said to Abraham he needed to obey what Sarah said to him. This has been used as an indication of her leadership role: Even to the extent that the word for 'obey' in the Hebrew (or, listen to) has been used elsewhere of Abraham's obedience to God (Genesis 22:18). This comparison of course giving more emphasis to the way Abraham and men should pay attention. In context this is seen to refer to a particular situation in which Sarah was right. Not something to hold as a truth in general. The same is true of any marriage. One partner may be right and the other wrong at any moment where the Lord would, if heard, want the wrong partner to obey the other in that situation (Luke 14:26 comes to mind as the prime allegiance to hold). This is not a reason or call by God to obey in all things (at all times). Jesus is full of grace and truth and any disciple of Jesus is called to follow Him in that (John 1:14). So as the Luke and the John passage together indicate righteousness with mercy should always come first. As the late Elim minister John Barr used to teach as regards 'truth versus error': *to make the exception the rule is deception*. So in specifics it was right for Abraham to obey Sarah or any man a woman in a similar event. This does not mean man should obey woman in general or, even the other way around if the occasion arises: even to the extent of a wife being perfectly correct in disobeying her husband e.g. A man saying worship an idol to his wife should not be obeyed (Deuteronomy 13:1-3).

> But God said to Abraham, "Do not let it be displeasing in your sight because of the lad or because of your bond-woman. Whatever Sarah has said to you, listen to her voice; for in Isaac your seed shall be called." *Genesis 21:12*

The passage shows Abraham is to obey Sarah. The context shows the extent to the obedience. What God was specifically referring to.

> . . . Sarah . . . said to Abraham, "Cast out this bondwoman and her son; for the son of this bondwoman shall not be heir with my son, *namely* with Isaac." *Genesis 21:9-10*

Women professing godliness: proclaiming the way of God to others

In 1 Timothy 2:10 we find Paul saying:

> . . . which is proper for women professing godliness . . .
>
> *1 Timothy 2:10*

This verse has been explained in terms of the verb 'professing' giving an emphasis of proclaiming or 'offering promises'. The idea is thus given that since it is godliness which is professed then it is talking about 'proclaiming the way of God to others' through prophesying and teaching.

The verb is seen in this way when it is compared with passages using this verb. So, let's take a look. The passages mentioned are Romans 4:21, Titus 1:2 and 2 Peter 2:19.

> . . . being fully convinced that what He had promised He was also able to perform.   *Romans 4:21*

> . . . in hope of eternal life which God, who cannot lie, promised before . . .   *Titus 1:2*

> While they promise them liberty . . .   *2 Peter 2:19*

The verb in these passages is *epangelló* and is seen here as a promise uttered. As the last passage shows, where it is used of religious teachers offering a way of salvation, it can indeed be understood to mean something uttered or taught. The problem arises when you see the whole of the verse and the immediate context.

> . . . in like manner also, that the women adorn themselves in modest apparel, with propriety and moderation, not with

braided hair or gold or pearls or costly clothing, but, which
is proper for women professing godliness, with good works.

1 Timothy 2:9-10

The natural emphasis in this context involves the idea of what
women who claim to fear God should be doing to show
that. If they say they are believers then they should do this.
It is proper for such to dress appropriately and to also work
at doing good. The emphasis is not what they are saying
(teaching or prophesying) and the act of saying it, though it
can be stretched to mean that and not incorrectly. Instead
the emphasis is on their life which they proclaim as believers.

'there is neither male nor female'

One of the most prominent passages used to suggest there is
no difference between men and women in Christ is Galatians
3:28.

There is neither Jew nor Greek, there is neither slave nor
free, there is neither male nor female; for you are all one in
Christ Jesus.   *Galatians 3:28*

By a reading of the context of this verse what is made clear is
that reference is being made to the inheritance available in
Christ and has no application given to roles or importance
of genders (this is brilliantly discussed in *Leadership Is Male*
by J. David Pawson 1988, published by Highland Books
Pages 54-56).

It is just like when Jesus spoke of the rain and the sun as a
benefit to both the wicked and the good (Matthew 5:45). This
does not mean the wicked and the good are equally valuable

as members of society. The inheritance we have in Christ has no boundaries, but it has no reflection upon roles and responsibilities, let alone differing callings on earth. This passage does not therefore bear immediate bearing on the issue of women or men in leadership. Not all men are fit for leadership which therefore helps see this.

If I said "There is no difference between Jew nor Greek, slave nor free, male nor female in regards to the air we breathe nor the water we drink", then no one would be taken seriously in suggesting this means therefore we can use this sentence in support of women in leadership.

Galatians 3:28 of course is not about the air we breathe, nor the water we drink. But, it is about something we all share and have in common: our inheritance in Christ. That is all that passage is about: Hence the context.

> If you *are* Christ's then you are Abraham's seed, and heirs according to the promise.   *Galatians 3:29*

Wives, submit to your own husbands
This is taken from Ephesians 5:22

> Wives, submit to your own husbands, as to the Lord.
>   *Ephesians 5:22*

I include this here in that as well as finding things out of context (eisegesis – things read into a text) I also found errors of accuracy which also contributed to my not trusting other parts of writings of authors for women in leadership. Here, a note was made by the author to the effect that the verb "submit" is not in verse 22, but is supplied from verse 21. The Greek is as follows:

28

hai - gunaikes - tois - idiois - andrasin - hòs - tò – kuriò

Ephesians 5:22

the - wives - to the – their own - husbands - as - to the - Lord

N.B. "ò" is for the Greek letter Omega as opposed to "o" for Omicron.

Similarly elsewhere "é" is for the Greek letter Eta and "e" for Epsilon.

This Greek text indeed appears to show that statement to be the case. But, this is not the Greek Text from which all Bibles are translated. The KJV, NKJV, Young's, etc are not translated from this one. The above is based on a text which lays heavy emphasis in its composition to two Greek manuscripts which when discovered at the end of the 19th century served to help the liberal thinkers of the day (a personal subjective remark on my part). These two codices disagree with each other and are in such good condition they are to be questioned as to their reliability as held by the readers of the day. Until printing in the West centuries later, all common reading material was handwritten and regularly copied when the material on which it was written wore out. Anything in good condition can only either be a fresh copy or not trusted as reliable. There are other such like arguments, but the fact is the Received Text which is closer by far to the Majority Text, in itself a close consensus of the majority of Greek manuscripts gives us the following:

hai - gunaikes - tois - idiois - andrasin - hupotassesthe - hòs - tò - kuriò

Ephesians 5:22

the - wives - to the - their own - husbands - submit yourselves - as - to the - Lord

I did not therefore find helpful to read that 'the verb *submit* was not in verse 22 but is supplied from verse 21'. Incidentally the sentence in Greek does not make complete sense in the 'utilised version' of the author in question: A further indicator as to the possible unreliability of the Greek text. In grammar, for a sentence to be real, it has to make complete sense.

In Genesis 1 both sexes are made in the image of God

This understanding is not uncommon and the truth contained in it is that both bear the image.

To say that both are fully made in the image however runs counter to a number of other scriptures.

> Then God said, 'Let Us make man in Our image, according to Our likeness . . .' So God created man in His *own* image; in the image of God He created him; male and female He created them. *Genesis 1:26-27*

This could give the idea that both sexes are made in the image of God, but this seems to run counter to Paul's words as follows.

> . . . a man indeed ought not to cover *his* head, since he is the image and glory of God; but woman is the glory of man . . . *1 Corinthians 11:7*

It is of note that the words Paul uses here give the emphasis on a wife being the glory of her husband. But, the idea is clear also that man here is seen as the image of God in contrast to the woman. Further when Jesus speaks of marriage as originally intended He says:

> . . . Have you not read that He who made *them* at the
> beginning *'made them male and female,'* and said, *'For*
> *this reason a man shall leave his father and mother and*
> *be joined to his wife, and the two shall become one flesh'?*
> So then, they are no longer two but one flesh. Therefore
> what God has joined together, let not man separate.
>
> *Matthew 19:4-6*

This makes little sense if the appreciation is that the first
man was distinct and separate from Eve when created. It is
the very act of God forming Eve from Adam which makes
this passage about marriage relevant. Having been divided
up he is one flesh again and complete with Eve. In other
words as a man, before Eve was made, he is understood as
being both male and female and able as such to reproduce.
A hermaphrodite being like most flowering plants are. The
living testimony to that remaining in mankind is that all men
have an X and a Y chromosome in every cell whilst all women
have two X chromosomes. This explains the immediate
reading of Genesis 5.

> This is the book of the genealogy of Adam. In the day that
> God created man, He made him in the likeness of God. He
> created them male and female, and blessed them and called
> them Mankind in the day they were created. *Genesis 5:1-2*

This could be understood to say he made mankind consisting
of men and women, but due to the specifics above the
emphasis is on the first man being made in this way. To
stretch it beyond that and suggest that woman is not a bearer
of the image of God at all would equally be inaccurate. This
can be seen by James' words.

> . . . no man can tame the tongue. *It is* an unruly evil, full of
> deadly poison. With it we bless our God and Father, and
> with it we curse men, who have been made in the similitude
> of God.
> *James 3:8-9*

Since the word used for "man" here is *anthròpos* it refers to
people in general: Both men and women. It is the word Jesus
used every time He called Himself the Son of Man: Since He is
not the Son of any particular man, but of the Race of mankind.
The other word for "man" *anér* is discussed in chapter 12
entitled *1 Corinthians 11:3* and also in the 1st Appendix.

So it is understood in scripture that woman bears the
image of God but, in some way, not to the same extent as
a man does. This makes the reference in Genesis 1 to a full
equality of the image of God inaccurate when the other
references are seen: In particular Paul and Jesus' references.
Therefore the context of the whole scripture differs from that
understanding. It is fair to say however that the differences
in regards to God's image in the genders are not explicitly
given us and thereby any further extension of this thinking is
fruitless to edification or learning. All one can safely say is
that both bear the image of God.

A man shall . . . cleave unto his wife:
cleave is used of the weaker cleaving to the stronger

It is argued that the Hebrew for 'cleave' of Genesis 2:24
dabaq, is used 'almost universally' of the weaker cleaving to
the stronger.

> Therefore shall a man leave his father and his mother, and
> shall cleave unto his wife . . .
> *Genesis 2:24 KJV*

The example given to show this is as follows,

> . . . cleave unto the LORD your God, as ye have done unto
> this day.
> *Joshua 23:8 KJV*

And Psalm 91:14 was also given,

> Because he hath set his love upon me, therefore will I deliver
> him: I will set him on high, because he hath known my
> name.
> *Psalm 91:14 KJV*

Now, some of you reading this will have had a 'double-take'
☺. The reason of course is that 'cleave' is not in Psalm 91:14
and for that matter, neither is *dabaq* in the Hebrew. What's
worse is the writer of this argument was quoting a previous
mention by another author for women in leadership without
checking it for themselves: This other author having been
even more emphatic in the 'almost universal' use of the word.
It turns out this second author was in turn using an older
source of which I have also obtained a full text.

The occasion in Joshua is 1 of 8 such instances where
dabaq is used for 'cleaving unto God' out of a total of 28.
This is as translated in the KJV. There are about 25 other
words or phrases it is translated into. It is used of 'cleaving'
to an array of things. Here are 4 further examples.

> And there shall cleave nought of the cursed thing to thine
> hand . . .
> *Deuteronomy 13:17 KJV*

> Moreover he will bring upon thee all the diseases of Egypt,
> which thou wast afraid of; and they shall cleave unto thee.
> *Deuteronomy 28:60 KJV*

> . . . if ye do in any wise go back, and cleave unto the
> remnant of these nations . . .   *Joshua 23:12 KJV*

> And they lifted up their voice, and wept again: and Orpah
> kissed her mother in law; but Ruth clave unto her.
> *Ruth 1:14 KJV*

So, in these examples we can see, in order, of cleaving unto
cursed things, diseases cleaving unto Israel, Israel cleaving
to the nations around and, Ruth cleaving to her mother in
law. Therefore it can be said that cleaving from *dabaq* is not
in any way used to make or show a degree of importance of
one to the other, but just and only the action of sticking/
glue-ing/cleaving 2 different parts together. Which is why in
Genesis 2:24 the verse ends like this:

> Therefore shall a man leave his father and his mother, and
> shall cleave unto his wife: and they shall be one flesh.
> *Genesis 2:24 KJV*

Being 'one flesh' clarifies the desired emphasis of sticking
together and has nothing to do with the weaker cleaving to
the stronger.

Paul's statements are his advice and not commands from the Lord

This is an important statement to make and is further attested
by the fact that Paul says this very thing in places. What is
needful is to clarify which passages they apply to and thereby
what examples these then give for today and, which are
clear scriptural principles to follow universally. Here is Paul's
'situational advice':

> No longer drink only water, but use a little wine for your stomach's sake and your frequent infirmities. *1 Timothy 5:23*

> I could wish that those who trouble you would even cut themselves off! *Galatians 5:12*

> But I say this as a concession, not as a commandment. For I wish that all men were even as I myself. But each one has his own gift from God . . . *1 Corinthians 7:6-7*

Timothy's personal need and the Galatian's 'troublers' are clear particular specific situations. Paul tempers his advice on marriage by stating this is his concession and not the Lord's commands so here also the issue is specific. It is claimed however a similar rule of wisdom as opposed to the Lord's authority is given in 1 Timothy 2:11-12.

> Let a woman learn in silence with all submission. And I do not permit a woman to teach or to have authority over a man, but to be in silence. *1 Timothy 2:11-12*

Paul does not say this though. Nor is it understood as non-universal, let alone cultural nor historical in significance when the next two verses are given.

> For Adam was formed first, then Eve. And Adam was not deceived, but the woman being deceived, fell into transgression. *1 Timothy 2:13-14*

The creation order and the fact that before the fall woman in her make up allowed her to be deceived are not separate situational, cultural or, historical specifics, but of universal important value.

And so

As I looked again at the things I read which had not persuaded me in the time before I turned from my stand against women in leadership, I was struck by the volume of good things I had previously missed. Yes, as shown there were passages misused and abused. But, there were several I ignored also. Even if it was not the prime passages which were the 'pillars' of the previous stand: Since I found none to explain these in a manner to give freedom for movement but, more on those later.

There is a spiritual principle (little known?) which involves one's choice. It is that once you make a 'stand', a particular choice on a matter, the mind and one's spirit is shut to the alternative. Only serious thrusting truth aimed directly at the 'pillars' of this chosen belief can change that. Unless the believer has decided to hold his beliefs in a position looser than scripture itself, like the Bereans of Acts 17, then there is little seeing of another position possible. This is a spiritual truth. It is something which can be ascertained from the fact that heresy - a bad doctrine or, set of teachings is a work of the flesh.

> Now the works of the flesh are evident, which are: . . .
> dissensions, heresies, envy . . . and the like; of which I tell
> you beforehand, just as I also told *you* in time past, that
> those who practise such things will not inherit the kingdom
> of God. *Galatians 5:19-21*

Now other versions of the bible have this translated as 'factions' (NIV), 'they separate into parties and groups' (GNB), 'party spirit (factions, sects with peculiar opinions, heresies)' (Amplified), 'party intrigues' (NEB), 'the feeling that everyone else is wrong except those in your own little group-and there will be wrong doctrine' (LB), all from the one word in Greek *hairesis*. Now, if I wanted to translate into Greek the English word 'heresy' there is no other to use. But, it is closely associated with the verb 'to choose', in Greek *haireō* (though there are limits to such linking as briefly explained within Appendix 4). There is a point however whereby once a teaching has been perceived that a 'choice' is made to believe it for oneself and it is from that 'choice' onwards that nothing persuades you away from it until it is removed again by an act of will to hold it again loosely. That is the spiritual truth I was referring to. This is the danger we all face with doctrine and belief and why it is important to have the 'Berean attitude' and to recall the Lord's injunctions to Christians:

> I counsel you to . . . anoint your eyes with eye salve that you may see.
> *Revelation 3:18*

To this end I have included here a prayer borrowed from my article entitled *The Characteristics of Deception* (readable at www.jarom.net):

> Dear Father,
>
> Thank you that you are Light and in you is no darkness at all.
>
> I ask that you shine your light in me and reveal all the beliefs and thoughts which I have taken on board as if from you, but in reality are not of you. I want to believe what is from you and nothing from the enemy. Just as you asked the church at Laodicea to anoint their eyes with eye-salve

that they may see, so I ask that you anoint my eyes that I may see. I thank you that the Holy Spirit will guide into all truth. I ask for discernment and courage to unlearn wrong things received as well as prevent new things which attempt to make a home in me. Help me to recognise any fresh work of the enemy which attempts to divert me from your ways.

Thank you that you give wisdom freely to those who ask.

Father I ask all this in Jesus' Name,

Amen

(1 John 1:5; Revelation 3:18; John 16:13;
James 1:5-8; John 16:23)

4

PAUL & DECEPTION

A text out of context is a pretext.
J. David Pawson

I have warmed to this saying by David Pawson ever since I first heard him say it. Of course he may not be the first to have said it, if so I do not know who is; he is the first person from whom I have heard it. There is so much misunderstanding of scripture, due to passages read and understood without consideration for the whole text out of which they arose, let alone the whole of the scriptures relating to a topic in hand, that they have indeed been pretexts for believing all sorts of weird and wonderful things. Much error and deceit arises out of such practise. In the end you find people believing what they want to believe and gather teachings around them according to that. This is where Paul's "itching ears" comes to mind.

> For the time will come when they will not endure sound doctrine, but according to their own desires, *because* they have itching ears, they will heap up for themselves teachers . . .   *2 Timothy 4:3*

The topic of 'women in leadership' and 'women teaching men in general' is no exception to this practise. But just when you think there would be somewhere, someone, who spent energy to unravel one particular context relating to the issue, you find very little. In fact, the opposite is found, because this context or facet of the issue is discarded as having little relevance in reality. I am referring to the singular and, in my appreciation, probably *the biggest reason* for Paul's writing on the subject: that of deception. Paul alludes to and refers to deception more than any other as his cause for saying what he says about women's public roles in the Church. Second to this issue, since the whole is in contrast to male involvement, is the issue of the creation order. But, in his mind deception is the biggest 'deal' here.

PROBABLY THE BIGGEST REASON FOR PAUL'S WRITING
ON THE SUBJECT: THAT OF DECEPTION.

I will attempt in this chapter to explain why this is so important to Paul and indeed to the Church. And though this is a separate chapter you will find my referring to this issue on a number of other occasions throughout the book. Paul, after all made very clear where our real enemy lies and where the attention of our enmities should be.

> We do not wrestle against flesh and blood, but against principalities, against powers, against the rulers of the darkness of this age, against spiritual *hosts* of wickedness in the heavenly *places*. *Ephesians 6:12*

The world of Satan and demons and all these entities was very real to Paul. He says they are the core 'beings', for Christians, to consider as enemies.

Deception and the role of women

Paul's reference and allusion to deception and the activity of the enemy relating to the issue of women's roles is plentiful. In 1 Corinthians 11:

> . . . because of the angels. *1 Corinthians 11:10*

I believe because of Paul's other references to deception practised by the enemy in regards to his writings on a woman's public activity that this is thereby a reference to fallen angels. All the spirit beings known as 'the enemy' are recognised as angels who have left their first estate and rebelled against God: i.e.

> . . . the angels who did not keep their proper domain, but left their own habitations . . . *Jude 6*

There are other views relating to what Paul might have meant by '**because of the angels**', but this is the most likely due to Paul's very regular emphasis on the issue of deception. I devote further chapters to show this in regards to the following passage:

> Let your women keep silent in the churches, for they are not permitted to speak; but *they are* to be submissive, as the law also says. *1 Corinthians 14:34*

As explained in those chapters the root issue is the way Eve was deceived, it is thereby an allusion to deception as the main reason. Please note, in my laying stress on the issue of deception now, the answers to how these are dealt with, I also cover in due course. The classic and the most direct reference to deception in regards to this subject is found in 1 Timothy 2:

> And Adam was not deceived, but the woman being deceived, fell into transgression. *1 Timothy 2:14*

So there we have it, the three main passages – 1 Corinthians 11, 1 Corinthians 14 and 1 Timothy 2 – where Paul has written about the roles of women and which in themselves are the 3 that have been used to decide about limitations as to their leadership or in teaching roles in public church life, have allusions or direct reference to deception. And yet deception itself has not been addressed fully as the main or a particularly important issue by many writers on women in leadership. Yet this is a vital context to cover. I would even say that anything that has been decided on the matter of roles of women without reference to the proper handling of the issue of deception is straying from Paul's intent.

Why was Paul so concerned about deception?

So, why was Paul so concerned about this? The answer lies in his personal understanding and appreciation to its relevance. His understanding is what led him to speak often about the topic. His constant effort to raise awareness of this is evident.

> I fear, lest somehow, as the serpent deceived Eve by his craftiness, so your minds may be corrupted from the simplicity that is in Christ.   *2 Corinthians 11:3*

> For such *are* false apostles, deceitful workers, transforming themselves into apostles of Christ. And no wonder! For Satan himself transforms himself into an angel of light. Therefore *it is* no great thing if his ministers also transform themselves into ministers of righteousness, whose end will be according to their works.   *2 Corinthians 11:13-15*

Now the Spirit expressly says that in latter times some will depart from the faith, giving heed to deceiving spirits and doctrines of demons . . .   *1 Timothy 4:1*

. . . all who desire to live godly in Christ Jesus will suffer persecution. But evil men and impostors will grow worse and worse, deceiving and being deceived.   *2 Timothy 3:12-13*

These are a few of his mentions of deception. This understanding of Paul's ranged from the deception attributed directly to the involvement of the enemy as the first and third of the above quotes show, to people that deceived others as per the second and last quote and, right onto deception due to one's own involvement with sin which Paul says involves all of us:

For we ourselves were also once foolish, disobedient, deceived, serving various lusts and pleasures, living in malice and envy, hateful and hating one another . . .   *Titus 3:3*

This interest and understanding of different types of deception, but particularly his appreciation of how the enemy does this directly is what is involved in his references within the passages relating to the roles of women.

Paul's own experience of deception?

It is Paul's own experience which led him to realise how important it is to be aware of the issue of deception. His own story reveals the matter. We first hear of Paul when the Church began in Jerusalem. He was known as Saul of Tarsus at the time. He was not a Christian, but instead an enemy of

Christians. Stephen, a deacon appointed to serve the needs of the church in Jerusalem was led to witness to Jesus. As a result, his opponents believing Stephen to be blaspheming and defiling the religion of the Jews, led Stephen out of Jerusalem and there they stoned him. Prior to his death there, Stephen testified that he had a vision of Jesus at the right hand of God:

> . . . and said, "Look! I see the heavens opened and the Son of Man standing at the right hand of God!" Then they cried out with a loud voice, stopped their ears, and ran at him with one accord; and they cast *him* out of the city and stoned *him*. And the witnesses laid down their clothes at the feet of a young man named Saul.
> *Acts 7:56-58*

That is the first mention of Saul. We then read a bit more.

> Now Saul was consenting to his death. At that time a great persecution arose against the church which was at Jerusalem . . . As for Saul, he made havoc of the church, entering every house, and dragging off men and women, committing *them* to prison.
> *Acts 8:1-3*

In his zeal to see the destruction of this new religion, Saul then set out to go further afield and see what he could do more.

> . . . Saul, still breathing threats and murder against the disciples of the Lord, went to the high priest and asked letters from him to the synagogues of Damascus, so that if he found any who were of the Way, whether men or women, he might bring them bound to Jerusalem.
> *Acts 9:1-2*

It was on the way to Damascus that the Lord appeared to him. Paul recounts this himself to others later in his life.

> Now it happened, as I journeyed and came near Damascus at about noon, suddenly a great light from heaven shone around me. And I fell to the ground and heard a voice saying to me, 'Saul, Saul, why are you persecuting Me?' So I answered, 'Who are You, Lord?' And He said to me, 'I am Jesus of Nazareth, whom you are persecuting.'
>
> *Acts 22:6-8*

Paul here recounts how he heard for the first time that the very Lord he had been trying to serve was Jesus and that he had been persecuting Him. Paul continues.

> Now those who were with me indeed saw the light and were afraid, but they did not hear the voice of Him who spoke to me. So I said, 'What shall I do, Lord?' And the Lord said to me, 'Arise and go into Damascus, and there you will be told all things which are appointed for you to do.' *Acts 22:9-10*

Recognising of course, but not fully understanding what was happening, Paul calls Jesus Lord and enquires what he must now do. He is told to go on to Damascus which as he said he was near. And that there he would be told further what to do. I now use the first mention of the whole event earlier in the book of Acts, to relate what happened next.

> Then Saul arose from the ground, and when his eyes were opened he saw no one. But they led him by the hand and brought *him* into Damascus. And he was three days without sight, and neither ate nor drank. *Acts 9:8-9*

Paul fasted for three days and nights without food or drink nor any light: Since he was unable to see. This time was a precious and important time as he sought to understand what had happened. To realise what had been going on. How could he have been wrong all along? How could he have been persecuting the very God he had been seeking to serve? These are very natural questions in the middle of this. We then read of how the Lord sent a disciple named Ananias to pray for Paul.

> And Ananias went his way and entered the house; and laying his hands on him he said, "Brother Saul, the Lord Jesus, who appeared to you on the road as you came, has sent me that you may receive your sight and be filled with the Holy Spirit." Immediately there fell from his eyes *something* like scales, and he received his sight at once; and he arose and was baptized. And when he had received food, he was strengthened. Then Saul spent some days with the disciples at Damascus.   *Acts 9:17-19*

Paul was converted and he was healed. To testify to this he was baptized and in staying with the disciples he learned more about Jesus. We learn later, that he in fact did not go to Jerusalem straight away after leaving Damascus. Paul relates this in his letter to the Galatians.

> . . . nor did I go up to Jerusalem to those *who were* apostles before me; but I went to Arabia, and returned again to Damascus. Then after three years I went up to Jerusalem to see Peter, and remained with him fifteen days . . .
>
> *Galatians 1:17-18*

Paul did not immediately launch into full ministry after his conversion, but sought to learn and understand more of what had happened that he should have been wrong. He learned about this and about Jesus as the Christ. He quickly learned about Jesus as the Son of God and testified to Him as that, but not all about what had happened until later. We read of his immediate witness as follows.

> Immediately he preached the Christ in the synagogues, that He is the Son of God. Then all who heard were amazed, and said, "Is this not he who destroyed those who called on this name in Jerusalem, and has come here for that purpose, so that he might bring them bound to the chief priests?" But Saul increased all the more in strength, and confounded the Jews who dwelt in Damascus, proving that this *Jesus* is the Christ.
>
> *Acts 9:20-22*

When he was fasting and praying for three days it was natural for him to recall to memory all the Old Testament scriptures relating to the Christ and as soon as he saw and was with believers he would have heard more about Jesus and made quick sense of these passages: So much so that he was straightaway able to witness to Jesus as the Christ, the very Son of God. But, it would also have been natural for him to question why he had been blind to this truth. What was it that had caused him to be so blindly persecuting the very Lord he desired to serve?

This was a firsthand encounter with the power and effects of deception. The genuine and real belief that you are doing God's will, when in fact you are doing the opposite: The belief in something 100% as right and good and true, when it is not. For that is deception. This is a spiritual condition. We know Paul did not persecute out of malice or evil intent, but out of a clear conscience for he testifies to this himself.

> . . . Men *and* brethren, I have lived in all good conscience before God until this day.   *Acts 23:1*

This included all the harm he was doing to the first believers. He did it out of a good conscience before God. Another way Paul describes it is as follows:

> . . . I thank Christ Jesus our Lord who has enabled me, because He counted me faithful, putting *me* into the ministry, although I was a blasphemer, a persecutor, and an insolent man; but I obtained mercy because I did *it* ignorantly in unbelief.   *1 Timothy 1:12-13*

Paul testifies that whilst he was persecuting Christians God accounted him as faithful: In the full knowledge that his actions were done out of a true heart motive for God. But, in his mind ignorant of the truth and unbelieving in that. And it was this love for God seen which was converted into a prayer to the Lord to set Paul up on the road to Damascus to call him out of this deception: Which is what Paul describes in Romans Eight. But that is a different topic and I deal with it in my publication entitled *Romans 8:28 in context*

So we see that Paul had first hand experience of what it was like to be zealous for God, but believing lies whilst understanding them to be the truth. This is a definition of deception. This is a direct work and influence of the devil and his minions. Paul understood that spirits teach these lies and cause individuals to believe they are receiving instruction from the Lord.

> . . . some will depart from the faith, giving heed to deceiving
> spirits and doctrines of demons . . . *1 Timothy 4:1*

This is what deceiving spirits do. They make you believe that
they are the Lord speaking to you. And we know the classic
passage:

> . . . we do not wrestle against flesh and blood, but against
> principalities, against powers, against the rulers of the
> darkness of this age, against spiritual *hosts* of wickedness in
> the heavenly *places*. *Ephesians 6:12*

It was to all believers, men as well as women to whom he
wrote:

> . . . I fear, lest somehow, as the serpent deceived Eve by
> his craftiness, so your minds may be corrupted from the
> simplicity that is in Christ. *2 Corinthians 11:3*

Deception as a topic became from then on an intricate part
of his teaching.

The experience of Deception enabled
Paul in his writings

This gave Paul an insight and understanding of how it was
that Eve was led astray in the garden. And why also he is
clear in his accounts that the first to sin is Adam, even
though it was Eve who first physically ate of the fruit. Eve
did not do it out of a bad conscience, but in deception. In
sincere belief she was doing something good.

> . . . through one man sin entered the world . . .
>
> *Romans 5:12*

Adam was conscious that his deed was wrong and against the command. Eve was not. This understanding by Paul is what enabled him to give the kind of instruction in how to teach others who are deceived:

> . . . a servant of the Lord must not quarrel but be gentle to all, able to teach, patient, in humility correcting those who are in opposition, if God perhaps will grant them repentance, so that they may know the truth, and *that* they may come to their senses *and escape* the snare of the devil, having been taken captive by him to *do* his will.
>
> *2 Timothy 2:24-26*

By patient humble step by step instruction led by the Spirit the very truths that can set the captive free are sown in the heart of the deceived. Out of my own experience of deceiving spirits and appreciation of their methods I have used this method to speak to many Jehovah's Witnesses over the years. Let alone fellow Christians led up the garden path or, following another red herring. For I have been there myself. Empathy and understanding for another often comes out of having been through it oneself. The issue of deception becomes important to the one who has learned of it, following freedom from its grasp.

Paul's references to deception

It's importance to Paul is seen by his many mentions of the word 'deceived' and allusions to it in many of his writings several of which I have already quoted: Acts 20:28-29 the elders at Ephesus; Romans 1:29 **'deceit'**: part of a list regarding the unrighteous; Romans 3:13 **'deceit'**: part of the sin of the wicked; Romans 16:18 '**deceive**': part of a warning against those who; 1 Corinthians 3:18 '**deceive**': Let no one deceive himself: 'don't kid yourself'; 1 Corinthians 6:9 '**deceived**': don't be since; 1 Corinthians 15:33 '**deceived**': don't be since; 2 Corinthians 4:2 '**deceitfully**' handling the word; 2 Corinthians 11:3 '**deceived**' (quoted above); 2 Corinthians 11:13 '**deceitful**' (quoted above); Galatians 6:3 '**deceives**': if, then; Galatians 6:7 '**deceived**': don't be since; Ephesians 4:14 '**deceive**': beware; Ephesians 4:22 '**deceitful**': old man corrupt; Ephesians 5:6 '**deceive**': let none; Colossians 2:8 '**deceit**': beware of those; 1 Thessalonians 2:3 '**deceit**': we were not; 2 Thessalonians 2:3 '**deceive**': let none; 2 Thessalonians 2:10-11 '**deception**': amongst the wicked; 1 Timothy 2:14 (quoted above); 1 Timothy 4:1 (quoted above); 2 Timothy 3:12-13 (quoted above); Titus 1:10 '**deceivers**': there are so look out; Titus 3:3 (quoted above).

Is it any wonder then that we find Paul being the one who points to deception as an issue probably more than any other? Is it any wonder the understanding he had of this issue relating to the female gender is also his prime concern?

The answer to deception

The answer sometimes given to deception is education. But this is not so. The answer to active deception is not education, but dedication to truth with a teachable heart. There is a difference.

You can know more than anyone else in your church, but be deceived about various things. You can be so intelligent, clever and full of facts and figures and still be 'led up the garden path'. Deception is a spiritual state. It is a veiling of the eyes to a balancing truth. It is, believing sincerely a truth out of context. It is, holding something as of God which is not, in entirety. Education per se is not the answer to such things. This is why Jesus was able to say...

> ... I thank You, Father, Lord of heaven and earth, because You have hidden these things from the wise and prudent and have revealed them to babes. *Matthew 11:25*

Education and knowledge feed the mind, but the heart is not moved but by the Spirit. Jesus' words were spirit and life. It is a combination of knowledge and life giving Spirit. The former is helped by education, but the latter only by sincere desire for truth in the heart: an honest desire for righteousness.

Deception involves either or both of these missing in measure. Education in itself involves teaching of knowledge. Without the heart's honest opening for truth and righteousness, it is insufficient to deal with deception. This is why Paul's reference to deception is not about women being unlearned. Men are unlearned too!

Deception and the gender difference

There is a difference between men and women in regards to deception. It is about the female make up and it is about the male make up. In particular with reference to how new information is processed. For women it is to do with the emotional reaction to new input: The overwhelming sensations which override decision making processes. This is what happened with Eve.

Woman's greater emotional sensitivity than man is a great asset to her, but in the area of desire type deception, renders her more vulnerable than man. Man's greater mental aloofness is an asset to cold planning, but his thinking base renders him more vulnerable in the area of decision based deception. It also makes him communicate differently and be more remote when he is not permitting a healthy operation of his feelings.

I will explain further in later chapters by highlighting the main example in scripture the deception Paul had in mind when referring to women. Allow me first to make the enemy's activity relevant to each of us a little clearer.

5

WHICH s/SPIRIT ARE YOU LISTENING TO?

Further explanation on the mechanics of deception

Deception, it is often thought, you should
counteract just by education.

This is not so

The most educated and wise people
are amongst the deceived

P aul understood deception from his experience. Many readers will find this subject unfamiliar territory and in the light of this it is needful to explain further the importance of this matter. A further foundation for the understanding required to Paul's writing on women in a church gathering.

We are told by John:

... test the spirits ...   *1 John 4:1*

This is a chapter about the need to do that and a little on how.

First, I will split hairs. When I say "Which s/Spirit are you listening to?" it could be understood, don't listen or, do not hear, but what I am after explaining is, don't go on to obey the voice of the enemy. And by the enemy of course I am referring to demons or evil spirits: whichever you prefer to call them. **It is ok to hear them; not to heed them.**

I will explain how it is ok to hear them. We know that in the wilderness Satan tempted Jesus:

> . . . Jesus was led up by the Spirit into the wilderness to be
> tempted by the devil.   *Matthew 4:1*

So from this we know two important things relevant to this discussion. One is that it is not bad to hear (listen in that sense) the enemy speaking to you. And second, if Jesus was talked to by the enemy then we should expect it too. It is what you do with what he (the enemy) says, that is important.

In the Christian life and even more so, in the Spirit filled Christian life, sensitivity to the spiritual is heightened. By Spirit filled I am referring to the baptism in the Holy Spirit and I have written separately about that in my article *What is Baptism in the Holy Spirit?*

This increased access to spiritual things to the mind of a person causes a greater hearing of things: both from the Lord and from the enemy. What tends to happen is without discernment the enemy is often mistaken to be the Lord speaking and thus the person will get involved in (sometimes) good things at the expense of the best. Or, the person is made to do something ahead of a proper 'natural' time. That is very common. Let alone all the other more usual stuff from the enemy like enticement to sin or influence to believe false doctrine (1 Timothy 4:1). Or, worry attacks, fear attacks leading to panics and anxiety, guilt attacks leading to condemnation, etc . . .

So does the enemy speak often to us?

Often is misleading, regularly is more accurate: Yes, I believe so. When Jesus was tempted in the desert as mentioned above this was a one off special occasion, but we are then told:

> And when the devil had ended all the temptation, he departed
> from him for a season.   *Luke 4:13 KJV*

This was one season only. But, there were more. Indeed when Peter spoke to Jesus and against what He had just been explaining, Jesus perceived the enemy at work and He said,

> Get behind Me, Satan! You are an offense to Me, for you are not mindful of the things of God, but the things of men.
>
> *Matthew 16:23*

Jesus knew how to test the spirits and only just a few moments after complimenting Peter on hearing from the Father, He now instead told him off for uttering from another spirit.

James tells us how to respond to the enemy's voice:

> Therefore submit to God. Resist the devil and he will flee from you.
>
> *James 4:7*

When you resist the enemy, you are refusing to accept what he says, he then flees. But, don't be fooled into thinking he is gone for good. It will only be the current season in which you have fought that he flees from. Jesus said,

> A disciple is not above *his* teacher, nor a servant above his master.
>
> *Matthew 10:24*

Of course this is a reference to persecution and the fact that what Jesus endured we are not to expect to be exempt from. But I believe as the above passages show that this is also true of the enemy's access to us, when he attempts to influence us: his speaking in order to divert us from God and His ways. He tried it with Jesus and he tries it on with us. So our job is as Paul put it, to be:

> . . . bringing every thought into captivity to the obedience
> of Christ.   *2 Corinthians 10:5*

The enemy speaks to us just like the Lord through the means of our thought life. To our minds, through dreams sometimes and, through other's words: as the example with Peter and Jesus above. What Paul just wrote is good to help us see this is a spiritual battlefield involving the mind:

> For the weapons of our warfare *are* not carnal but mighty in God for pulling down strongholds, casting down arguments and every high thing that exalts itself against the knowledge of God, bringing every thought into captivity to the obedience of Christ . . .   *2 Corinthians 10:4-5*

It is the thought life that is the battleground. And it is our responsibility to take captive every thought not in line with Jesus.

The challenge

Once it is recognised that the enemy is involved in this activity of feeding the thought life, then the practise is to go against what he says.

So, the remaining issue now is one of discernment. How do you recognise it is the enemy, or the Lord, or just your very own thoughts?

These are the three main activities prevalent in the mind. How can you tell which is whose?

If the hurdle is passed that the enemy does regularly have an input in the lives of Christians, just as he did with Jesus: it happens regularly to all Christians, then the remaining issue is to discern the voices and then heed the good one and resist the bad one: Knowing how to deal with these things. So as John put it we need to:

... test the spirits ...   *1 John 4:1*

The simplest and easiest way is to know what is being said and line it up with what is known as right and wrong. If the feeling is of hate and desire to murder, then of course that is wrong and needs to be resisted. That is the means to kick out such a feeling. By resisting it and deciding that is not what you want in your life. This is effectively what the Lord told Cain right at the beginning:

If you do well, will you not be accepted? And if you do not do well, sin lies at the door. And its desire *is* for you, but you should rule over it.   *Genesis 4:7*

By resisting the sin's call to act you disarm its hold on you. It is of note that sin is personified in what the Lord said to Cain. My understanding of this is more in terms of evil spirits identifying with a particular sinful activity than the deed itself being a type of person. Either way, it is resisting the feeling, the urge, the overriding influence or pressure to do evil which is the crux. But, conversely by heeding it you are less able to overcome later as you have welcomed it. It thereby begins to make a home in you. However, your ability to return or resist is never removed fully: it may be hidden and quenched as Paul said, but it is always there to some extent. Paul spoke of this ability being severely hampered in terms of a conscience sealed up:

> ... having their own conscience seared with a hot iron ...
>
> *1 Timothy 4:2*

And Jesus spoke of what 'one had' as being taken away. This signifies that 'we all had it' in the first place. So our use of it enables our retention of it. I will need to expand on this: to explain it. Jesus said:

> For whoever has, to him more will be given, and he will have abundance; but whoever does not have, even what he has will be taken away from him. *Matthew 13:12*

This is in fact a fundamental principle. So important, that Jesus is quoted 5 times as saying it in the gospels. But is it preached about? Is it understood? Not very much is the answer.

At first glance it appears unfair. If you have something more is given you, but if you have nothing what you do have is removed. But it is not material things Jesus is referring to. It is a spiritual principle. And this principle – this law if you will – is important in establishing an effective means of discerning what the enemy says to you as a believer. Indeed deception, it is often thought, you should counteract just by education. I have already stated and will again, this is not so. The most educated and wise people are amongst the deceived. This is because the enemy has been listened to and the matter is not just intellectual, but spiritual. The answer to deception is education with a right attitude of heart: with the right type of desire for truth in the heart. Education on its own is not the answer.

So what is Jesus referring to?

He is referring to the desire in the heart to do what is right,

WHICH S/SPIRIT ARE YOU LISTENING TO?

to sincerely knowing the truth, to truly love God. If you have this, then more ability will be given you and you will have abundance. But, if you do not have pure motive in your heart, what you do have – even your very ability to choose – will appear unusable as you enter the realm of deception. It will still be with you – the freedom to choose – but your heart will cause you not to see, to be blinded thus not able to choose the good from the bad. This is why Jesus taught in parables:

> . . . Lest they should see with their eyes and hear with their ears, lest they should understand with their heart and turn, so that I should heal them.   *Matthew 13:15*

Jesus knew the ability remained, but because of their inner choice to not desire the truth: their motives being impure, in order to "respect that" freedom, He spoke in parables thus it was their own hearts that prevented them from understanding and turning.

But, Jesus turned (in His speech) to His disciples and then said:

> But blessed *are* your eyes for they see, and your ears for they hear . . .   *Matthew 13:16*

So the first step to effective discernment is having the right heart. This is why James started the mention of resisting the enemy with humbling yourself before God first.

> Therefore submit to God. Resist the devil and he will flee from you.   *James 4:7*

If this is a regular practise in your daily life then, you are doing this first step anyway. If your daily habit is to spend time with your God, then you are in a place of humility before your God which is of value in this matter: If not all the way through your day, at the very least at that part of your day. This then enables the Lord to highlight what the enemy may have put your way. Your spirit may be spoken to by the Lord. At all times the enemy may speak, the Lord however is into having a relationship and as such needs to be invited, welcomed, asked; not assumed upon. He has self-control; the enemy does not. So that He will not always speak immediately into a situation if not asked.

> . . . the fruit of the Spirit is love, joy, peace, longsuffering, kindness, goodness, faithfulness, gentleness, self-control . . .
>
> *Galatians 5:22-23*

Not only is this useful to know about God – that He has self-control – and thus how important it is we spend time with Him, but it is a valuable aspect of recognising the enemy when he speaks. What the enemy says will not involve self-control on his part. He will pressure, cajole, squeeze, with a thought or feeling to get you to do or believe something. The Lord will not. The Lord instead returns to mention something again (though to a limited amount of times). This latter point is relevant in that if you do not want to hear Him, the Lord will also not go on.

JESUS LEADS HIS SHEEP; HE DOES NOT 'DRIVE' THEM!

But His heart remains the same, so if you do seek His face you will find Him repeating what He may have said a long time ago.

... many are called, but few are up to it. *Matthew 20:16 JM*

> See my booklet *The meaning of eklektos*
> for the translation: few are quality

The call remains the same, but often the fulfilment does not occur or is not seen since the response to the call is down to the individual. So pressure to do something which does not allow for your choice is invariably the enemy trying to influence you. If he can't wait for a day to do this thing, then it is not normally the Lord. This is the spirit of the voice I am talking about: A regular facet of the enemy's ways. But the Lord does at times require us to act quickly and do something within a brief time frame. Usually in these times it is our personal fear or laziness that prevents us to act. It normally involves our conscience and thus is God's speaking revealed. The enemy does not use the conscience; he uses guilt. There is a difference.

These are useful aspects to know when trying to recognise what is going on in our minds, our hearts, our feelings . . . Sometimes these things are too strong, or they feel that way. But, if in doubt just say, 'Lord. I am not sure this is you, I will wait a while'. He will understand. If it is Him, He will then open your mind to a passage of the bible or something that will encourage you to understand this is Him. If not, anything the enemy gives extra will also with it have a 'pressure' indicator. You must because it needs to happen now to prove things, etc...

It is the opposite with the Lord because,

> ... where the Spirit of the Lord *is*, there *is* liberty.
>
> *2 Corinthians 3:17*

There is freedom, release where Jesus is. There is peace and He is gentle.

> Come to Me, all *you* who labour and are heavy laden, and I will give you rest. Take My yoke upon you and learn from Me, for I am gentle and lowly in heart, and you will find rest for your souls. For My yoke *is* easy and My burden is light.
> *Matthew 11:28-30*

So the thought, the word or suggestion received can be discerned as to what source, what spirit is speaking by the tone and manner of voice. It is the fruit of the voice that tells us the source. Pressure, compulsion is the enemy's; conviction, gentle persuasion is the Lord's.

The important thing is to sincerely desire righteousness, talk to God with absolute honesty with Him and yourself, asking for His help and then watch for the tell-tale pressure or the simple conviction and inspiration. If in doubt wait, quieten your heart and soon the tone will tell the source. But, don't be fooled in thinking the enemy never speaks. He does regularly. But so does the Lord.

A powerful weapon

Just as Jesus used the Scripture to respond to the Devil in the wilderness, so the bible is like a sword and is most effective in resisting the enemy once he is recognised as speaking or trying to influence. If you do not know a scripture to 'speak into' your current situation ask the Lord for one. How you receive that is also important to recognise. The enemy loves to string passages together – usually out of context – to 'convince' the person of his cause. I recommend my article

The Characteristics of deception to help in recognising that type of scripture giving. If you have been following such a 'string' of passages for some time and do not know it, you may find my article *Making an idol* useful in recognising such. I will leave you now with a verse that I have often found helpful to fight with:

> . . . seek first the kingdom of God and His righteousness, and all these things shall be added to you.   *Matthew 6:33*

6

AS GENESIS 3:16 ALSO SAYS – A DISCOVERY

An initial look into 1 Corinthians 14:34

My attention was drawn to Genesis 3:16 by a cross-reference. When reading 1 Corinthians 14:34 attached to the words '**the law**' there was a letter-mark corresponding to a note in the margin. This referred to Genesis 3:16 in the KJV I was reading.

> Let your women keep silence in the churches: for it is not permitted unto them to speak; but *they are commanded* to be under obedience, as also says the law*.
>
> *1 Corinthians 14:34 KJV*
> **Genesis 3:16*

The obedience which women are to practise, as mentioned in the law, refers to Genesis 3:16. This is the appearance that the cross-reference gave. I diligently read the Genesis passage and, what seemed possibly relevant was the last portion of this verse.

> Unto the woman he said . . . and thy desire *shall be* to thy husband, and he shall rule over thee.   *Genesis 3:16 KJV*

This is the Lord speaking to Eve following the eating of the forbidden fruit. Now here also was a note in the margin. This note corresponded with the words '**to thy husband**' and this read, '**Or, subject to thy husband**'. Not a reference to another passage this time, but an alternative rendering of the translation. Making the passage read:

> . . . and thy desire subject to thy husband, and he shall rule
> over thee. *Genesis 3:16 KJV & margin*

This translation dispenses with the added words which had been placed in italics: '*shall be*': Italics is a method used by bible translators to show words that are not in the original language, but added to help the flow of meaning. The alternative rendering dispenses with these '*added words*'.

What interested me is how this fitted in with the immediate context of the passage.

The Lord mentions to Eve to do something with her 'desire' such that her husband is to make a ruling. The only other 'desire' mentioned in Genesis 3 is that of Eve's for the tree of the knowledge of good and evil. Meat indeed! I began to see with this rendering an understanding of what Paul was saying.

However before I really go there and discuss this fully I wish to highlight the importance of 'finding' this Genesis 3:16 passage.

As the law also says

As we saw 1 Corinthians 14:34 tells us '**as the law also says**' in the midst of a passage instructing women in church gatherings:

> Let your women keep silent in the churches, for they are not
> permitted to speak; but *they are* to be submissive, as the law
> also says. *1 Corinthians 14:34*

Women, Paul says here, are to keep quiet in churches. Let's not forget though that from previous verses he says women are able and free to pray and prophesy publicly. We know this for in talking about women in public gatherings he had already said:

> . . . every woman who prays or prophesies with *her* head uncovered dishonours her head . . .   *1 Corinthians 11:5*

In chapter 12 I explain the mention of a woman dishonouring her head refers to her husband. But, since women are free to pray and prophesy publicly, when Paul says they are not to speak he is talking about something else: something specific. He is referring in part as shown by the next verse to the asking of questions whilst in a public gathering.

> And if they want to learn something, let them ask their own husbands at home . . .   *1 Corinthians 14:35*

That is the immediate context: the following verse expands on what it is that is not to be spoken in the public setting. Paul gives a similar context in his first letter to Timothy,

> Let a woman learn in silence with all submission.
> *1 Timothy 2:11*

A learning event is seen as explicit in both places.

In 1 Corinthians 14:34 and 1 Timothy 2:11 we see learning by women as something important to Paul, but one that requires them to be quiet and submissive, that is in public gatherings. He says they are to be silent whilst in a learning situation. That is the context. This submission we saw is something which Paul alludes to as given in the law.

. . . they are to be submissive as the law also says.

1 Corinthians 14:34

The Law

Paul's use of the phrase '**the law**' is of interest since everyone could look that up and see what he is referring to: Why this should be. The authority by which we can also pay attention to, since Paul is using it that way.

However there appears to be very little if anything in the scripture Paul was using – our Old Testament – which 'says' that women are to be submissive. So much so that other writers have expressed that the bible is not what Paul was referring to, but instead the Jewish Oral Law of the day. Jewish regulations based on ancient sources – precepts forming instructions on ceremony and civil activity as transmitted through verbal teaching hence its name, the Jewish oral law. For example Charles Trombley in his book on the topic of women and teaching says:

> Josephus, a well-known Jewish historian who said he was a Pharisee, wrote, "**The woman, says the law, is in all things inferior to the man. Let her accordingly be submissive.**" He referred to the oral law, not the Bible as "**the law**". It's the same law referred to in 1 Corinthians 14:34-35.
>
> *Who Said Women Can't Teach?* by Charles Trombley Page 29
> Published by Bridge Publishing Inc. 1985.
> Josephus' quote is from *Apion II*, 201.

Charles Trombley also quotes J.F. Schleusner, a German lexicographer:

The expression '**as also saith the law**' refers to the Oral Law of the Jews now called the Talmud.

ibid. Page 23 quoting:
The Tyro's Greek Lexicon Published by Brown and Greek, 1825.
Both quotes used with kind permission of Bridge-Logos,
Orlando, Florida USA
1-800-631-5802

Question:

Can it really be believed that Paul in writing to a Gentile church was advocating Jewish Oral Law as a guide?

I don't think so. Here is my reasoning.

In all of Paul's writings we find this phrase '**the law**' almost exclusively to speak of 'the law of Moses' i.e. the Pentateuch, the first five books of the Old Testament.

The exceptions are when he used a particular argument without the phrase needing general appreciation of it other than as 'the rule' or, 'the guide': in these different senses. These excepted mentions are self-explanatory in their own passages. They are,

. . . the law of faith.	Romans 3:27
. . . the law of my mind . . .	Romans 7:23
. . . the law of sin . . .	Romans 7:23
. . . the law of the Spirit of life . . .	Romans 8:2
. . . the law of sin and death . . .	Romans 8:2
. . . the law of righteousness . . .	Romans 9:31
. . . the law of Christ.	Galatians 6:2

So, of about 120 *other* references to '**the law**' Paul speaks about the Law of Moses. That is to say: Genesis, Exodus,

Leviticus, Numbers and Deuteronomy. For even though the law as given to Moses at Sinai is only contained in parts of those books, and indeed, mainly the last four, all five are understood to be referred together as 'the law' section of the Hebrew scriptures. Indeed the Jews' scriptures have often as a whole been referred to as 'the law and the prophets'.

Thus, when it says in 1 Corinthians,

> ... women ... *are* to be submissive, as the law also says.
>
> *1 Corinthians 14:34*

It is very reasonable to expect that we find a specific command that women are to be submissive somewhere in '**the law**': somewhere in the first five books of the Old Testament, the Torah. But where is this statement, where does God say to woman to be submissive in any way?

Well, in Genesis, Exodus, Leviticus, Numbers, and Deuteronomy we 'appear' to find nothing of the sort. There is a possible allusion to it in Numbers 30, but there is no clear statement by God which seems to be shown 'to say' to women to be submissive in any way in '**the law**'. That is, when we look at the majority of Bible translations/versions. However, I believe that when we look at the Hebrew text direct, we find the answer in the second part of Genesis 3:16.

> ... unto your man your desire and he to rule over you.
>
> *Genesis 3:16 Hebrew literal*

It is my belief that this is what Paul refers to when he says '**as the law also says**'. I have yet to demonstrate conclusively this is the case, but as I unravel it's meaning and uncover good sources of evidence, it is my aim that the reader will go on to agree with me Genesis 3:16 is not only the prime candidate, but is the true source material to appreciate where Paul was coming from. Since the mention of '**the law**' by Paul in 120 places does refer to the biblically contained 'law of Moses' it is my belief that the Bible – of the day – is what was referred to in 1 Corinthian 14:34. So what is the setting for Genesis 3:16?

7

AS GENESIS 3:16 ALSO SAYS – A REBUTTAL

The setting of the law – this command

What I have expressed thus far is this: The woman is told by God,

> . . . and thy desire subject to thy husband, and he shall rule over thee.
> *Genesis 3:16 KJV & margin*

And about the setting I have said that the Lord mentions to Eve to do something with her 'desire' such that her husband is to make a ruling. The only other 'desire' mentioned in Genesis 3 is that of Eve's for the tree of the knowledge of good and evil.

Now since the Lord is speaking to Eve after the event of eating the forbidden fruit, and due to that, it seems reasonable to link the two instances together. Even if the word for 'desire' itself is a different one in the Hebrew, they both involve a 'feeling for' something. However the word for desire in God's utterance is more forceful in nature: it is the word 'teshuqah' and it is also found in Genesis 4:7 and Song of Solomon 7:10.

> If you do well, will you not be accepted? And if you do not do well, sin lies at the door. And its desire *is* for you, but you should rule over it.
> *Genesis 4:7*

> I *am* my beloved's, and his desire *is* toward me.
> *Song of Solomon 7:10*

According to Strong's the word here for 'desire', *teshuqah* involves a 'stretching out after': a longing. At its root the word *shuq* is found and this means 'to run after': i.e. Overflow . . .

(Strong's: Concordance and Dictionaries by James Strong, Madison N.J. Copyright 1890)

So the desire God talks to Eve about is not just some casual wish or feeling for something, but a more overflowing hankering after type of desire. Something that will tend to overwhelm the senses is the impression one receives. It is this strong type of desire God is saying to woman to do something about.

Genesis 3:16 & 4:7

The intensity of the desire can easily be appreciated in Song of Solomon. It is between two lovers, the amorous strong sentiment well described and recorded in that book: A great source of inspiration for love songs and poetry.

But in Genesis the two passages where *teshuqah* is found have given rise to a mixing of their meanings and purposes. It has been said that sin's desire in Genesis 4:7 is also the kind of wrong desire involved in 3:16. That is to say one passage being imposed on the other. Various authors have done this and give the appearance of copying each other.

Part of the reasoning is that both passages have very similar grammatical construction:

> **"unto your man your desire and he to rule over you"** of Genesis 3:16

appears similar to:

> **"unto you it's desire and you to rule over it"** of Genesis 4:7.

However, there are sufficient differences to remove any such cross-linkage of meaning. It is a shame the similarities have been highlighted and left there, to give the impression that there is, indeed equally strong evil implications in both passages, as regards the desire of the woman, whilst in fact the differences in my view far outweigh and nullify this linkage. The idea is false that since sin spoken of and personified in Genesis 4:7 – which as shown has a desire and because it is sin, a desire evil and malevolent – this must mean that the desire in Genesis 3:16 is also evil and malevolent.

The differences provide the rebuttal needed

To help demonstrate the very real and important differences between Genesis 3:16 and Genesis 4:7 I have produced two diagrams which portray the elements of each passage. They picture well the differences and remove any idea that woman's desire is the same as sin's desire in anything other than perhaps intensity.

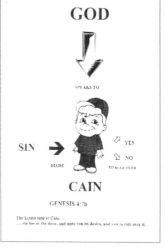

The person spoken to by God in Genesis 3 is the one with the desire and in Genesis 4 the one to whom the desire is aimed at. So that sin in Genesis 4:7 has no relationship to the woman in Genesis 3:16. Any linkage of this is false. Her desire is not sin's desire.

The person to decide in Genesis 3 is the man related to the woman – "your man" – and in Genesis 4 the person to decide is not related to sin until and if a decision is made otherwise. At this point sin only **"lies at the door"**. Sin has no link to the woman in Genesis 3.

To compare woman with sin because of similar grammar and a similar word found in both passages, when the type of desire is not in view, opens a door to blame woman for all kinds of evil: A most dubious method of interpretation. The differences already shown warrant severe doubt upon such dark and sinister imposition of desire which is like sin's upon a woman's. Indeed the context which I have begun to discuss does not warrant it.

What is similar in both passages is that the separate person spoken to by God needs to decide and overcome the feeling or desire's imposition. The will of the individual is seen as able to act independently of the desire. Such that in Genesis 3 the woman can submit it, and in Genesis 4 the person is to resist the Sin's desire to rule and thus be free from it. So for the theologically minded, free will as it has been named is therefore visible and a full blown reality in these two passages, and that, after 'the Fall'. I mention this again and expand on it briefly in the next chapter.

Judgment?

The idea that what God said to Eve is a judgment upon her,

a punishment of some sort I believe is also false. I aim to show this too in the following chapters. This judgment idea has been one of the premises upon which the similarities of Genesis 3:16 and 4:7 indicate both are mentions of conflict. Irrespective of the pointers to the differences between the 2 verses showing the link as unreal, the very foundation idea that Eve was being judged – in the form of a punishment – is further ground upon which the link between the two passages has been formed.

Three persons are addressed by God following the Fall: Adam, Eve, and the Serpent. Only the serpent is cursed and the next curse mentioned is that of the ground. Judgment in the sense of punishment is understood in the case of the serpent. I believe that what the Lord spoke to Eve and Adam was more for their ongoing benefit than a form of retribution. I go on to explain this benefit.

Indeed God's actions later in Genesis 3 show that the before mentioned death if they ate of the fruit was not carried out upon Adam and Eve. So, was this judgment in the sense of a punishment for Adam and Eve?

No, but instead a wise ruling which I shall explain more fully in the next chapter.

But I will finish this one by saying God's word is true, the pronouncements made to Eve and Adam respectively were not judgments, in the sense of punishments for sin, but something to help them. We can see this – immediately – is not about their sin since God took care of it already:

> God had said that in the day that they ate of the fruit of the tree, the consequence is that they would die (Genesis 2:17). The penalty had been already set and it was carried out in full. Death occurred that day. Blood was spilt. God is first on record to shed it (G.3:21): the first person to

kill. And doing so provided Adam and Eve with a covering and a full substitute to their own deaths.

It was the sacrifice of the animals whose skin God gave them to wear that meant blood had been spilt, thus showing the way forward to the One whose sacrifice – and Own blood spilt – Who would finally bruise Satan's head (G.3:15): Jesus Christ, the woman's Seed (Galatians 4:4).

God providing a covering for sin on that day was not thereby equally speaking judgment on this sin – as a means of punishment – to Adam and Eve. He was not calling for retribution on it twice. What God spoke into we shall now see in a better way.

8

AS GENESIS 3:16 ALSO SAYS – AN EXPLANATION

N ow that Genesis 3:16 is in view and it's false link with Genesis 4:7 understood, let's look at what it reveals. The literal Hebrew reads,

> . . . unto your man your desire and he to rule over you.
>
> *Genesis 3:16 Hebrew literal*

We have seen that this desire is an overflowing feeling for something. God is here instructing Eve to submit this desire to her husband in order for him to rule over. Adam as her husband is to make a ruling over the desire submitted to him. Now, let us suppose Eve in desiring the fruit, to that strong a desire, instead of eating it, she had in her conscience and memory the certain understanding that she needed to talk with Adam about it, would the fruit have been eaten?

This new practise thereby can be seen as a help to prevent further 'falls' whenever new attacks present themselves. It is not a curse therefore, but a new approach to help overcome an existing weakness. It is a help for the woman in the midst of her existing ability to feel inclined to do something new which may not be good. Would Eve had eaten the fruit if she had this appreciation in place?

A recognised ability

Well, it all depends on how she responds to her conscience first, and whether Adam did anything about it second. Both actions are required to prevent or stop the eating of the fruit. But clear ability within Eve is recognised by God. God sees this whilst a strong desire for something is in place. A desire such that you feel and believe it is good to do e.g. to eat the fruit. God knows whilst this desire is there, you still have the ability to decide. The ability to exercise your will in regards to this 'desire' before you do anything about it. Even if it is just to say, "Help!" God sees this faculty still alive and able to function in the middle of deception. Which is why, I believe He speaks to Eve about submitting it. It is also of theological note that this ability is also being seen by God after the event of 'The Fall'.

My mention of God recognising an 'ability' in woman or man after the Fall needs a small expansion. This is because a number of Christians have been taught something known as 'total depravity' or perhaps more accurately 'total inability' exists since 'the Fall'. As such to read on without addressing this would for any in that position mean they are left with a clear stumbling block to accept what is here. We looked at Genesis 4:7 and the differences existing with Genesis 3:16. Here too we can see the similarity that God saw an ability in Cain to overcome, if only he had been willing. So in this it agrees with Genesis 3:16. Jesus also saw an ability when he taught that if you have sin in your life, so attached to you that it is like your own eye or your own arm, you could cut it off (Mark 9:43-48). But, the crux here of course is sheer determination and complete desire to do so for it to occur: Hence, the illustration of the eye and the arm, so that only absolute resolve will do it, as it is either that or eternal death.

There are other passages, but a good one used to say total depravity exists is in fact pointing to the opposite:

> . . . you *He made alive*, who were dead in trespasses and
> sins . . .
> *Ephesians 2:1*

As it is, it is quickly visible as useful material to the idea that man is so depraved, so totally disabled that only if God brings fresh life in, will the dead be raised. This is therefore a very 'popular proof text' to say that total depravity is a truth of scripture.

However in this popular 'proof text' there is clear inherent ability alluded to. In English it reads ". . . **you *He made alive*, who were dead in trespasses and sins . . .**" This is read as saying that God made alive dead people: Folk with no life to respond to God with. Whereas actually the "**in**" here is only valid from the Greek original if understood 'whilst in'. This is because the Greek for "in" is *en*, but it is not found in this Verse. It can be found in the next Verse, but not this one. The reason it is used in English is that the words "**the trespasses and the sins**" as found in the Greek text are in a grammatical form known as the Dative. The use of the Dative here is to indicate *the means by which* they were "**dead**". This is known as the instrumental use of the Dative. It is whilst *active* in trespasses and sins that they "**were dead**" Clearly implying an *ability* to not be active in sin. Anyone now appreciating this grammar is unable with a clear conscience to use this verse to say there is total depravity, but the opposite.

GOING ON
A safety feature
This exercise of will then, in response to the knowledge of a strong desire (for something) being present, is a safety feature.

It is a safeguard against the enemy and any deception which occurs by means of a desire in the woman. But not just any old desire: An overflowing and imposing feeling: Something that impresses and pressurises the person to change direction or be forceful in an act and usually out of time.

This interpretation of the text of Genesis 3:16 is supported when one looks at the Septuagint – the Greek version of the Old Testament scripture – which Paul regularly quoted from in his writings: I have added a quick example of this use of the Septuagint by Paul at the end of this chapter.

In this version we read that '**thy submission shall be to thy husband, and he shall rule over thee**'. The Greek literally is '**thy turning shall be to . . .**' Since Paul regularly quoted from this version and we saw in 1 Corinthians 14:34 he mentions the book he quotes 'as the law says', it is this rendering the reader would have looked up. So the idea that Eve was from then on to submit her strong desire for a ruling by her husband is strengthened.

Now, if the husband is present and he recognises this desire is not within the scope of safe practise and says so – let alone against God's express command as it had been with Adam and the forbidden fruit – then, the woman in her exercise of will can overcome the desire and prevent her acting upon it. All this is dependent on the husband's activity being positive: his not being passive and just allowing things to happen. Something, which I wish to discuss further for 'there' is man's own difficulty or problem. His weakness involves passivity and it is this which the Lord deals with next in Genesis 3:17. This further new imposition by God – the curse on the ground – will then be an additional internal biblical witness to the ruling just given to the woman as for good. God is step by step speaking into the revealed weaknesses in both man and woman in order to help them overcome future attacks by the Enemy, the Serpent of old, Satan (Revelation 12:9).

We can begin to see then there is a disadvantage in the area of desire, the feeling for or, emotional side of a woman. If not handled by the woman it is a potential trap to bad belief, bad behaviour and a fall into sin. Any further attacks by the enemy can thus be equally damaging. This rule by the Lord therefore is not a punishment, but a safety net to help woman in her weakness. This is the same with what the Lord says to Adam next. It is not a punishment, but a safety net. But before I go there I wish to say what can be done if Adam had not been there.

What if the woman is alone?

Indeed what does a woman do with a strong desire like that, when her husband is either not there or, he is not playing his part in seeing and deciding about a possible danger? My advice is to wait. Waiting is an effective means of resisting the enemy. He wants something done there and then. He imposes and has no patience. Whereas the Lord will return to tell us something and He does not pressurise us. He leads His sheep; He does not drive them. He is not impulsive. Had Eve waited with the fruit, even if in her hand, the strength of desire would have subsided. The memory not to eat this fruit was already present, but not the strength of spirit to heed it. We know she knew not to eat it and remembered this. Adam had been given the command not to eat of that fruit and he had informed Eve. We know he had done this before because as soon as the serpent begins a dialogue with Eve about the tree she tells him what only Adam could have told her:

> . . . of the fruit of the tree which *is* in the midst of the
> garden, God has said, 'You shall not eat of it, nor shall you
> touch it, lest you die.'   *Genesis 3:3*

Now we do not know if the embellishment "**nor shall you
touch it**" is her own or Adam's when he originally told her,
but she knew and recalled the command not to eat. But in
the midst of the longing, without intervention, her acting
fully upon the desire causes her to transgress and fall in the
trap of the evil one. Deception is real and is to be guarded
against by both men and women in their personal lives
and in the church. Men too are subject to attacks and if
pressurised to believe or to speak or to act, again waiting is a
good tool to help discern the source of the impulse. As time
passes the spiritual influence to do wrong decreases not little
by little as if it was a leak, but as a sudden release of intensity at
a point when impatience kicks in by the giver of the intensity:
the enemy. Impatience is one of his fruits.

A note about sin

The reason why Adam was accounted 1st to sin though
he transgressed second is that he was not deceived. His act of
eating the fruit was wilful and thus in the clear knowledge
that this was going against God's express command.

Unlike Eve who, being deceived transgressed but was in a
sincere belief that what she was doing was good – i.e. – not truly
seeing what she was doing for what it really was, immediately
prior to the act - which is a good definition of deception.

Adam was not in this frame of mind and not deceived
but wilfully transgressed. This could be the reason for being
accounted first to sin. Eve was not accounted guilty until she

realised. There are various scriptures to show that God does not account sin (the guilt of) on someone if they definitely did not realise they were doing wrong (or, until they do).

> . . . through one man sin entered the world . . .
>
> *Romans 5:12*

Adam is accounted responsible for the first sin: whereas guilt of wrongdoing in the case of someone doing it unknowingly occurs when they realize it.

> . . . if he touches human uncleanness, whatever *sort of* uncleanness *it is* with which a man may be defiled, and it is hidden from him – when he realizes *it*, then he shall be guilty.
>
> *Leviticus 5:3*

> . . . if a person swears, speaking thoughtlessly with *his* lips to do evil or to do good, whatever *it is* that a man may pronounce by an oath, and it is hidden from him – when he realizes *it*, then he shall be guilty in any of these *matters*.
>
> *Leviticus 5:4*

Sin is not taken account of when there is no knowledge of wrongdoing.

> . . . until the law sin was in the world, but sin is not imputed when there is no law.
>
> *Romans 5:13*

Eve transgressed first, but as we saw she is not reckoned as the first to sin. She was blinded as to the law – the command not to eat – and by this deception carried out the act of eating the fruit first. She was deceived and God seeing this, then spoke directly to her regarding that in Genesis 3:16b.

Now to the weakness of man: a look at Genesis 3:17 as an internal witness to the things the Lord spoke to woman in Genesis 3:16 being for good and of value today, as referred to by Paul.

An example of Paul's use of the Septuagint

The Septuagint is the Greek Version of the Old Testament of our bibles. It was the version commonly used in New Testament times as Greek was the language that pervaded the world of the day. When Alexander the Great conquered the known world and then the Greek rule continued for a few centuries this language became the norm for commerce, administration and news. So much so that in 285-247BC in Egypt's Alexandria, Hebrew scholars got together to translate the Scripture of the Jews and compile a Greek translation. This is what is known as the Septuagint, a name based on the tradition that it took 70 scholars. It is the version quoted in our New Testament. So if you read a quote and wonder why it does not always read exactly like the Old Testament in your bible this is because 'your' Old Testament was translated direct from the Hebrew into 'your' language.

Paul wrote in Romans,

> Beloved, do not avenge yourselves, but *rather* give place to wrath; for it is written, *'Vengeance is Mine, I will repay,'* says the Lord. *'Therefore if your enemy hungers, feed him; if he thirsts, give him a drink; for in so doing you will heap coals of fire on his head.'* Romans 12:19-20

This quote by Paul is taken from Proverbs 25:21-22. The Greek in the Septuagint he relates is exactly the same as in the New Testament text. In 'our' bible the Proverbs passage reads,

> If your enemy is hungry, give him bread to eat; and if he is thirsty, give him water to drink; for so you will heap coals of fire on his head...
>
> *Proverbs 25:21-22*

Paul does not mention '**bread**' or '**water**', but he does say '**in so doing**'. The former is in the Hebrew text and not in the Greek; the latter is in the Greek Version, but not in the Hebrew. It is of note that where doctrine is affected by translation the Septuagint is not quoted by the New Testament writer. However, the very regular use of this paraphrase of its day, by Jesus and the apostles, is a help to encourage more readable versions today, if one does not forget the limits posed by non direct translation on dogma.

9

GENESIS 3:17
A REVELATION OF MAN'S WEAKNESS

With Genesis 3:16 in view, the false link with Genesis 4:7 put aside, and now a fuller understanding given, let's look at Genesis 3:17 to reveal man's weakness and thus help confirm the explanation.

Just as in Genesis 3:16 God speaks direction and help for the perceived weakness in woman, so also in Genesis 3:17 we find Him speak into Man's own weakness. In some respects this is more easily visible. This is because of other passages which add to and correlate with this event. But the value in being identified here is in its attestation to the series of acts by the Lord in Genesis 3 as helps, thus pointing further to Genesis 3:16 as relevant today. So I would like now to explain about man's own challenge, how God addresses it, and then how this affects the gender roles.

It will be noticed by the keen observer the only 2 curses mentioned in Genesis 3 are that upon the Serpent and that upon the ground. Nothing else is mentioned as cursed and neither is it implied. An accurate read reveals the whole as a help for onward life. What has not always been noticed or recognised is that the curse on the ground mentioned in Genesis 3:17 was also removed several centuries later.

About 17 centuries later to be precise. I am writing in the 21st century AD, though I started writing this book in the 20th. AD denotes 'Anni Domini' – the year of our Lord in Latin. Similarly I wish momentarily to use the letters AC to denote 'After Creation' (dispensing with the Latin). With that in place, I can say that in 1657AC the bible record, shows the curse on the ground was removed (This date is easily deduced from the accurate records given us in Genesis 5. One only has to make a chart and step by step add the details given whilst all the time accounting for the date from 1AC: a bit of fun). At the event of this curse removal upon the ground we are also given the original purpose or intent for that curse. The record of this occurs just after Noah and all with him – the 8 – left the ark following the Flood.

> Then Noah built an altar to the LORD, and took of every clean animal and of every clean bird, and offered burnt offerings on the altar. And the LORD smelled a soothing aroma. Then the LORD said in His heart, "I will never again curse the ground for man's sake, although the imagination of man's heart *is* evil from his youth; nor will I again destroy every living thing as I have done. While the earth remains, seedtime and harvest, and cold and heat, and winter and summer, and day and night shall not cease."
>
> *Genesis 8:20-22*

Here we find many important things said by the Lord: the promise of the seasons and, night and day, etc whilst the earth remains. But of course, this is not the space for highlighting everything here. Let us focus on the section relevant to our present discussion.

> . . . I will never again curse the ground for man's sake, although the imagination of man's heart *is* evil from his youth . . .
>
> *Genesis 8:21*

I wish to add here some words which were prophesied at the time of Noah's birth by Lamech his father. They relate to this event.

> ... he called his name Noah, saying, "This *one* will comfort us concerning our work and the toil of our hands, because of the ground which the LORD has cursed."   *Genesis 5:29*

It is of note that Lamech and his own father Methuselah – Noah's Grandad – the eldest man that ever lived and went on to be 969 years old, both died just before the Flood. And, if the book of Enoch is also anything to go by, then the building of the ark involved the whole family. Noah means literally "Rest" and Lamech in prophesying was looking forward to the rest for mankind when the curse on the ground would be removed. It appears that prophecy ran in the family. The book of Enoch is quoted in Jude 14-15 and the contents were referred to by Peter and Jesus: The 'Son of Man' is regularly mentioned.

The curse on the ground

It's all very well my mentioning the above, but I haven't yet quoted the passage where the very curse is initially brought into effect. Here is the whole section.

> Then to Adam He said, "Because you have heeded the voice of your wife, and have eaten from the tree of which I commanded you, saying, 'You shall not eat of it': Cursed *is* the ground for your sake; in toil you shall eat *of* it all the days of your life. Both thorns and thistles it shall bring forth for you, and you shall eat the herb of the field. In the sweat

> of your face you shall eat bread till you return to the
> ground, for out of it you were taken; for dust you *are*, and to
> dust you shall return."   *Genesis 3:17-19*

So, we have now seen twice the mention by God that the
curse on the ground was for man's sake. Also the Genesis 8
mention amplifies the meaning for us of what is meant by
'for man's sake'. There the Lord said,

> . . . for man's sake, although the imagination of man's
> heart *is* evil from his youth . . .   *Genesis 8:21*

The Lord is saying that "although" the imagination of man's
heart is evil from his youth, He is removing this curse which
is for man's sake. In other words, in spite of the imagination
of man's heart being evil from his youth God is removing the
curse from the ground. This tells us therefore the purpose
for the curse on the ground. It was to hinder in some way
the outcome or the activity which the evil imagination could
produce. It is an expansion upon the saying that this curse
was done for man's sake. It is also of note here that this is
specifically mentioned as for man's sake. It is not for woman's
sake. What has this got to do with the events leading up to
The Fall? Why should God feel able to remove this curse and
cease it's function?

Man's weakness

When Eve ate the fruit out of the deception connected to
the desire for the tree she also involved Adam.

> So when the woman saw that the tree *was* good for food,
> that it *was* pleasant to the eyes, and a tree desirable to make

94

> *one* wise, she took of its fruit and ate. She also gave to her
> husband with her, and he ate. *Genesis 3:6*

It is of note and important indeed to see that Adam is described as being with her. We know, since it is clearly recorded that Eve was deceived. This is not the case for Adam. Which is probably why, as I mentioned he is the first to be accounted to sin. What Adam did was wilful and he was conscious to its importance. Now picture what things would have been like if Adam, since he was with Eve, had spoken up to her about the fruit being forbidden. He could have helped remind Eve as to what God actually said and that he would rather trust God who had never given him cause to doubt what He had said before. Or, that she should not eat this fruit since he certainly would not and that already her feelings in her desire were clouding her judgment. Why not wait a while and see if she still feels like it later rather than impulsively act.

Now, all this spoken by Adam would have required concerted mental activity on his part. He would have to be active in thinking through his words and thus see to his will acted upon verbally. However, Adam is not recorded as doing any of that, but the opposite. He is seen as in a state of passivity. Of letting things happen. He is seen as mentally lethargic. Passivity as a state of mind and heart is thereby the revealed weakness in man.

Edmund Burke a prominent Irish author and statesman of the 18th century said 'all that is necessary for the triumph of evil is that good men do nothing'. It was apt in the garden, it is relevant in many relationships, let alone in every society, ever since. Who has to be reminded of the little jobs overdue for being done? Who has no prompting required for 'their own' pet projects or hobby horses? But, a task for another is in a different league? And so on.

So, what do we see God do to address that – To prevent further passivity allowing evil to make a home and grow? We see Him cursing the ground for man's sake. And what is a curse. It is a living and active force to cause the thing uttered. In the case in hand it involved the ground producing thorns and thistles. It would now require man's constant activity to overcome this difficulty in order to have food. This would cause his passivity to be overcome.

Let us not forget that for the next 17 centuries following the initial curse on the ground man was still not permitted to be a carnivore, or more accurately an omnivore since both would be permitted. This was only allowed after the Flood following the removal of the curse from the ground. And of course, after all living things had been destroyed in the Flood including the previous abundant vegetation. Which means that very little edible vegetation would have survived. This helps us to appreciate Lamech's sentiment when he said, **"Noah . . . will comfort us concerning our work and the toil of our hands, because of the ground which the LORD has cursed"**. From now on, vegetation was no longer going to be sufficient to provide food to eat. Here is the record of God's permission to eat meat:

> Every moving thing that lives shall be food for you. I have given you all things, even as the green herbs.   *Genesis 9:3*

What would limit evil now?

God removed the curse from the ground which had prevented the passivity in man to allow evil by the activity to overcome the difficulties the curse on the ground had brought. This gone what prevented the growth of wickedness?

New restrictions

The Flood not only caused the death of everyone who walked the earth except for 'The 8', but it was the means by which God transformed the landscape and inhabitation of Man. The continents were split, new mountain regions emerged, new seas, new rivers, deserts, etc. It is a whole topic in itself. Now after the Flood, man's wickedness was limited within the new boundaries given him. Food was still going to be a challenge, but not to the same extent. Crossing rivers, mountains, deserts and oceans were now new and more abundant obstacles. Some things remained like the river Euphrates (Genesis 2:14 – its mention there recognises its existence later). But, God was to bring even more restriction: more limitation upon the growth of wickedness. For that to happen He waited until the population had grown sufficiently so that when men gathered together in a fertile plain to enable their common activity, He could then impose a further restriction upon the growth of wickedness. This was confusion by means of different languages. This occurred at the tower of Babel incident as the place was then called (literally: *Confusion*, Babylon).

> Therefore its name is called Babel, because there the LORD confused the language of all the earth; and from there the LORD scattered them abroad over the face of all the earth.
>
> *Genesis 11:9*

All these new restrictions in place meant that the curse on the ground was not required and the course of history could now develop as the Lord preferred when compared with the pre-Flood existence. Of course, the recognition of these actions, by God has far reaching implications in the world of theology and doctrine. The belief in the God of the Bible's having absolute foreknowledge effectively challenged. But this also is not within the scope of this book. I recommend my article *Evil and God's knowledge* for the interested.

Passivity is the man's challenge, but this is in contrast to the woman's since her emotional strength can at times be an asset to get a job done which man is slow on the uptake about or to persevere in. Of course it also must not be forgotten that if an evil man desires to sin passivity was the least of his concerns. Cain murdered his brother. But, if he had desired to do the right thing (righteousness) then, he would have been active in opposing the desire of sin upon him.

So, what is the difference between the sexes as relevant to this discussion?

I answer this briefly in the next chapter.

Objections to the curse removal addressed

To help concrete the interpretation that God removed the curse on the ground in Genesis 8:21 by removing some possible objections I offer the following:

> . . . and Jehovah saith unto His heart, 'I continue not to disesteem any more the ground because of man, though the imagination of the heart of man *is* evil from his youth . . .'
> *Genesis 8:21 Young's Literal Translation of the Holy Bible*

This verse as translated by Robert Young helps to show that by "**I will never again curse the ground**" as translated in the

NKJV, the meaning is more to do with 'I do not allow the curse to continue' then 'I will not do it a second time'. The latter understanding of course has the problem also of suggesting that doing a curse a second time is something perhaps necessary for God to do: i.e. cursing once by God is insufficient.

Some would say that a curse by God on someone is irreversible nor is a blessing from God irreversible. This would tally with the truth that a calling on someone's life does not change or a gift from God is not taken away as per Paul's words:

> For the gifts and the calling of God *are* irrevocable.
>
> *Romans 11:29*

In the KJV this is translated as "**the gifts and calling of God *are* without repentance**".

Which some have read to mean that a man need not repent to still have these, but the context refers to God not changing His mind. It is His repentance that is in view. So to remove such misunderstanding more modern versions have used the word 'irrevocable'. So this verse would support the view that a curse or a blessing from God on someone is irreversible.

However it is not a person or even a living entity that has been cursed in Genesis 3:17 and removed in Genesis 8:21, it is the ground. It is not someone, but an object for a purpose. This purpose is mentioned in both passages and it is that purpose for which it served that the curse was put there, and then removed. Something different was put in place to 'take care' of the purpose.

Now some will note that Robert Young does not translate the word 'curse' in his translation. This is because the word

Qalal has been used in the Hebrew as opposed to the word *Arar* in the earlier mention.

There are two main Hebrew words for 'curse', ARAR (62; also used for 7 other words a total of 7 times) and QALAL (41; also used for 27 other words a total of 40 times).

This shows that for both *arar* and *qalal* the prime use is for 'curse'.

Other words for 'curse' in Hebrew are ALAH (19), BARAK (4), CHEREM (7), MEERAH (5), NAQAB (6), QABAB (7), QELALAH (31), SHEBUAH (1), TAALAH (1).

Words used for 'curse' in Greek in the New Testament Anathematidz-o (3); Ara (1); Epikataratos (3); Kakologe-o (2); Katanathema (1); Katanathematidz-o (1); Katara (6); Kataraomai (6)

This is helpful in that the Greek translation of the Hebrew Old Testament translates both *Arar* and *Qalal* with the same root word in Greek katara in Genesis 3:17 and 8:21. Showing that for those translators the 2 passages in question meant a curse in the same way.

Now Quoting from both Hebrew words translated as curse in the case of Naaman it can be seen that they can also mean the same thing.

Translated from Qalal

> . . . they hired against you Balaam the son of Beor from Pethor of Mesopotamia, to curse you.   *Deuteronomy 23:4*

> . . . king of Moab, arose to make war against Israel, and sent and called Balaam the son of Beor to curse you.
> *Joshua 24:9*

. . . they had not met the children of Israel with bread and water, but hired Balaam against them to curse them. However, our God turned the curse into a blessing.   *Nehemiah 13:2*

Translated from Arar

And Balaam . . . took up his oracle and said: . . . Blessed *is* he who blesses you, and cursed *is* he who curses you.

Numbers 24:2-3, 9

Therefore please come at once, curse this people for me, for they *are* too mighty for me. Perhaps I shall be able to defeat them and drive them out of the land, for I know that he whom you bless *is* blessed, and he whom you curse is cursed.   *Numbers 22:6*

So, even though there is more of an emphasis in *qalal* to a curse as in swearing or demeaning someone's name, it can be readily seen it is used effectively in the stronger sense that *arar* mostly gives, that of a spiritual pronouncement with power.

Also it must not be forgotten to suggest God just merely speaks evil or denigrating (despising) the ground in Genesis 8:21 whilst He had cursed it (proper) in Genesis 3:17 is to say what? God doesn't like the ground? He despises it?

No, but instead it makes sense that in Genesis 8:21 just as in the examples just given of Balaam cursing using the word *qalal* it is equivalent and indistinguishable as *arar* within these contexts.

A final note about The Curse and curses in the bible

The world of doctrine and theology has made much use of 'The Curse' as it relates to salvation. The bible alone mentions many curses. Some explicitly like the one in question upon the ground. Some implicitly or inferred by the feeling that something bad is in itself a curse: these can include sin, death, the groanings of creation (as mentioned by Paul in Romans 8:22), etcetera. One specific curse removed – as discussed – does not infer the removal of any other real, inferred or imagined 'curse'.

Of course, if it is a personal curse you are mindful of or fretting about, then don't forget the following:

> Like a flitting sparrow, like a flying swallow, so a curse without cause shall not alight. *Proverbs 26:2*

10

THE DIFFERENCE BETWEEN MEN AND WOMEN

Of course the physical difference is not what is meant. What is the difference as relevant to our discussion? I would like to express the difference in view as follows:

WOMEN ARE EXPERIENCE ORIENTED
MEN ARE TASK ORIENTED

Research carried out on men and women changing nappies (diapers in America) showed men were significantly faster than women. The report on a survey was announced on Capital Radio on the 18th July 2004. It took 1 minute and 36 seconds for a man to change a nappy. It took 2 minutes and 5 seconds for a woman.

This is because as task oriented the guys were treating the operation as a kind of pit stop as with a Formula 1 racing car. Everything laid out in their minds so the job was speedily accomplished. The ladies however interacted more with the baby and as experience oriented this meant that the only pleasure in the task was that interaction.

Men tend to live in their heads more; women tend to live in their feelings more. This being observed we read that,

> . . . the woman saw that the tree *was* good for food, that it *was* pleasant to the eyes, and a tree desirable to make *one* wise . . .
> *Genesis 3:6*

Satan tempted Eve in the things which she experienced. The task of obeying the command was no longer in view. She was deceived.

> . . . the serpent deceived me, and I ate. *Genesis 3:13*

> . . . the woman being deceived, fell into transgression.
> *1 Timothy 2:14*

Now her experience of seeing the tree was there before she ate. Her experience of wisdom and food was yet to be until she ate. But the desire for the new combined with the existing made it real. Food she experienced and wisdom as good in general. Not yet for this fruit, but real in general. So hooks were in place which Satan used to entice her to choose to eat. All based on her experience.

Deception involves making a decision to believe something which is not wholly true. Satan wants us to believe something that is not true. But we believe it to be once we choose for it. He uses what we know to be true as hooks to add his lies to. To this he adds feelings or intensity that 'show' this is 'good' or 'important' or 'real' or 'immediately required' . . .

So, just as he used scripture to tempt Jesus in the wilderness, but always texts out of context, so he uses truths we know of, but only in part. Highlighting only the bit he wants in view. Please note that this method is the same for deceiving men and women.

The deception involving women in a gathering of believers where learning occurs therefore lies in the experience of what is being heard. Does it feel right? Nice? Are they comfortable? Does it agree with one's experience? Whether real or aspired to?

Of course these are not wrong in themselves. It is the time taken to discuss these and the diversions possible which are the issue: Not least because the feelings expressed or their intensity may only be temporary.

Deception and the gender difference

There is a difference between men and women in regards to deception. It is about the female make up and it is about the male make up. In particular with reference to how new information is processed. For women it is to do with the emotional reaction to new input: The overwhelming sensations which override decision making processes. This is what happened with Eve.

Woman's greater emotional sensitivity than man is a great asset to her, but in the area of desire type deception, renders her more vulnerable than man. Man's greater mental aloofness is an asset to cold planning, but his thinking base renders him more vulnerable in the area of decision based deception. It also makes him communicate differently and be more remote when he is not permitting a healthy operation of his feelings.

Marriage and the gender difference

If it is understood that women are more experience oriented than men and that men are more task oriented than women this is helpful in a relationship. This is a brief aside.

A man who aspires to make his task consist of the good experience of the woman in his life will grow to understand and appreciate her. The woman who communicates what is needful to help the man in her life in his task will benefit greatly. The man not being a woman will take time to learn what is needful, but if the woman shares what is needful even if only once then both will grow to appreciate and enjoy the life they have together . . .

11

THE CREATION ORDER &
MY TURNING POINT

In the early chapter entitled *The Status Quo* I mentioned the creation order as one of Paul's arguments for allegedly saying women are not to exercise authority over men or to teach. Writers for women in leadership – which I now am also – have stated the creation order involved the marriage relationship, but without giving clear evidence to demonstrate this. This I aim to do. But, allow me to explain how I at first saw Paul's creation order argument, then my 'turning', followed by good evidence for the marriage relationship's 'main use' of the creation order.

As translated in most bibles 1 Timothy 2:12-14 tells us that a woman is to be silent, not teach or exercise authority over man due to the creation order, let alone deception. Now as I read authors suggesting this order was only for the marriage relationship I disputed that. After all, since there was just one man and one woman in 'the beginning', neither a statement that the reason man came first meant something exclusively about marriage nor a statement that this was only a general gender situation were valid. Both are valid at that point. In that setting it is neither one nor the other of these, but something about both. Did not Paul after all use this order argument with a general gender use? In a discussion involving the wearing of a head covering? In the passage about head covering he said,

> For man is not from woman, but woman from man. Nor
> was man created for the woman, but woman for the man.
>
> *1 Corinthians 11:8-9*

Indeed he did. Or, appears to, for what exactly is meant here by an immediate reading of the translation does not show nor help to clarify this. I will help with this in a later chapter.

So for me thereby, the creation order was important to retain a 'male leadership' position. I was not alone, for Evangelical writer John Stott states in his book *Issues Facing Christians Today* (Marshall Pickering 2nd Edition 1990 pages 254-284) that for him 1 Corinthians 11:3 was indeed putting the emphasis on a general gender order to be understood.

> But I want you to know that the head of every man is Christ,
> the head of woman *is* man, and the head of Christ *is* God.
>
> *1 Corinthians 11:3*

So, although my take on things had begun to alter in providing safeguards and understandings by covering the argument on deception, as explained in preceding chapters, the creation order remained implacable in my mind.

And who was I to argue with God? It's His Word and the above passage does in that way seem incontrovertible.

But, since I was in a new research mode and enquiring further due to His call to look at this issue again, when I 'happened to' read a seemingly unrelated passage I had a sudden volte-face.

My 'turning'

When I came to Jesus in 1972 I had no upbringing into

theology or in any church setting for that matter and only had about two years of religious education lessons in the local schools. These in the norm of general religious studies included some of the Bible but I had been ignorant of its contents. It was a book of stories and boring at that point. Once I became a believer however this background served to help me take things I read in the bible at face value. I learned that there really existed a Devil. That pride was a sin. All about the miracles Jesus did. That was great! This of course led me to believe in God's power and willingness to heal today since I had no adverse theology to influence my reading of the text as it was presented.

In all this I learned about Creation and the God whom I was having a relationship with having done all this in 6 days. This is important for appreciating my 'turning' which I wish to describe. As someone interested in science I was intrigued as to how Creation fitted into or against the arguments of evolution which was taught in schools. The simplest argument I have ever heard was from the lips of the author and broadcaster Gerald Coates. It goes something like this: 'Which is easier to believe? That nothing made something out of nothing or, someone made something out of nothing?'

Even before I was a Christian, at a young age, I recall thinking to myself that if we came from monkeys then there must be around – somewhere – some monkey-type beings in the process of turning into men. I had heard of none. So, even back then, I had doubts as to this evolution teaching. I have since a full belief that 'science' has no problems with creation and following some research and reading into this I have produced some articles of my own. I recommend for those interested *From Nothing to Nature* by Prof. E.H.

Andrews (Evangelical Press) or for those more scientific *In Six Days* edited by John F Ashton PhD – a collection of 50 essays from Doctorate scientists (New Holland). Suffice to say the empirical evidence points away from evolution and to an intelligent, orderly, mathematical, inspiring position. I share this to show that the honest appreciation that the Creation occurred in a literal 6 days is a realistic one. It is the background to what happened next: My turning point.

I was reading Jesus' argument with the Pharisees as regards the use of the Sabbath, the day of rest.

> And He said to them, "The Sabbath was made for man, and
> not man for the sabbath. . ."   *Mark 2:27*

What then occurred is a thought. What Jesus was saying by "**The Sabbath was made for man . . .**" is that the reason, and sole purpose, for God creating in 6 days was as an example for man. What an awesome thought!

Let's not forget that Hebrew is the language of the Old Testament (except for a few small portions in Aramaic). This comprises the Genesis account of creation. Now, the Hebrew mindset and biblical demonstration is that the number 7 indicates a complete amount: Something whole. This also needs to be borne in mind. So this means that in the record that God took 6 days to create all there was a gap. There was a gap of 1 day to account for. It is 'the gap' which produced the feeling for an appreciation that 1 day in 7 is to be used to cease from work: A ceasing: To rest: the Sabbath.

The understanding of seven as a complete amount is in the very word. The following is distilled from Strong's and Young's analytical concordances. The word for 'seven' in

Hebrew is *sheba*. The root of this word is *shaba* which in itself is translated as 'to swear' or 'make an oath'. The idea is that it means to 'be complete'. So that to 'seven yourself' is as if to repeat a declaration seven times. A means of saying you are telling the 'whole' or 'complete' truth.

This awesome consideration, that God deliberately created in 6 days as opposed to 5 seconds or, 10 years or, whatever – in order to give an example – to the being in His own image, Adam, was in my mind.

It set me thinking.

What was therefore, the specific immediate context, for God creating woman after man?

If, the purpose was so simple, for creating in 6 days and as Jesus showed, any religious mindset 'adding to' this simplicity caused misuse and misunderstanding of the Sabbath, what would this say about the creation order?

On the day that Adam was put to sleep and woman was made from part of Adam this is what we are told:

> And the LORD God caused a deep sleep to fall on Adam, and he slept; and He took one of his ribs, and closed up the flesh in its place. Then the rib which the LORD God had taken from man He made into a woman. And He brought her to the man. And Adam said: "This *is* now bone of my bones and flesh of my flesh; she shall be called Woman, because she was taken out of Man." Therefore a man shall leave his father and mother and be joined to his wife, and they shall become one flesh.
> *Genesis 2:21-24*

This immediate passage says no more than that this event is to do with the one-flesh relationship. It is an example for the marriage relationship.

Just as, a few verses before, we read about the immediate purpose for the Sabbath as follows, so also as above can be read the reason for the creation order. The Sabbath is first mentioned as follows:

> And on the seventh day God ended His work which He had done, and He rested on the seventh day from all His work which He had done. Then God blessed the seventh day and sanctified it, because in it He rested from all His work which God had created and made. *Genesis 2:2-3*

This was my 'turning point'

I could not escape the simplicity and beauty, let alone the wonder that this was God's simple purpose for creating woman after man. As an example in the one-flesh relationship. What this fully meant in practise was something else.

I still had to learn and understand all that, but here was an open door to walk through into light. Further understanding was going to follow. Indeed as I set out onwards to make sense of things arising from this new foundation I had to learn New Testament Greek and do more research to remove the veils, the nuances and the errors from many translated versions of the Bible. I smile as I write this, because if I read someone else's work, and they had written that I would be on the defensive. A warning bell would have rung.

Of course this means I have my work cut out. I need to explain and demonstrate where and how mistranslation has occurred. I need to give sufficient backing information and in simple terms for this to be realised.

What I do hold to and have practised for a long time now is that the Berean attitude to 'check if these things are so' (Acts 17:11) is the only way to learn the truth and unlearn what is not helpful from one's own theological 'boxes'. This is what Paul advocated as regards prophecy and I also recommend of anything you read.

> Do not quench the Spirit. Do not despise prophecies. Test all things; hold fast what is good. *1 Thessalonians 5:19-21*

So, what about the 'John Stott verse', 1 Corinthians 11:3?

12
1 CORINTHIANS 11:3

The late John Wimber, founding leader of Vineyard Christian Fellowships was interviewed in the *European Christian Bookstore Journal* (August 1993 issue Page 35). On the topic of women in leadership he made brief mention that in his understanding women are prohibited in scripture from involvement in the government of the church; it is a gender issue. He said that prohibition comes primarily from three texts in the New Testament. This topic was only briefly covered and there was no mention as to which texts were involved.

As a reader familiar with the issue 'the three' passages immediately came to my mind: those contained in 1 Corinthians 11, 1 Corinthians 14 and 1 Timothy 2.

As previously stated John Stott in his book *Issues Facing Christians Today* discusses this topic. For him the main passage which prohibits women from governing in the church is that of 1 Corinthians 11; it is as far as I could see his 'final hurdle'.

Personally, as mentioned in the Preface I 'stood beside' David Pawson and his book *Leadership Is Male* for quite a while and would have certainly approved of John Wimber's thinking; but, following further research and a number of discoveries in the Bible texts relevant to the issue, I am now totally committed to a full role for women in leadership.

Allow me then to address the first text mentioned, that of 1 Corinthians 11: as far as the issue is concerned it primarily deals with a headship of woman by man due to God's creation order as encapsulated in verse three:

> . . . the head of every man is Christ; and the head of the woman *is* man; and the head of Christ *is* God.
>
> *1 Corinthians 11:3*

The significant portion is '**the head of the woman is the man**'
In the Greek text we find, *kephalé-de gunaikos ho anér*
That is, 'but/and head of woman/wife the man/husband'.
Like the French 'femme', in Greek there is only one word for 'wife' and 'woman', that of *guné*.

Equally for 'man' *and* 'husband' there is only one word, *anér*. It is from this word that we get the English 'android': a robot that looks like a man: like *Data* the brilliantly played android by Brent Spiner of *Star trek – The Next Generation*.

So that in order to know which word to translate into the English version, often the context will help clarify, whether a wife and husband is being mentioned as opposed to a woman and a man.

There is also another word for 'man' that of *anthròpos*. It is from this word that we get the English 'anthropology': the study of peoples.

What is the difference between *anér* and *anthròpos*? You may ask.

In my research, I have looked at every place where *anér* is to be found in the New Testament in whatever form it is found (see Appendix 1). By a different 'form' I mean whether it was in the singular or plural and in every declension for that word. A declension is an adaptation of a word so it looks different like *gunaikos* and *guné* as already to be observed above. These are an essential part of the New Testament Greek language.

Declensions in Greek

In English, if I said 'a man speaks to an angel.' it would mean something different to 'an angel speaks to a man.' This is because the order in the sentence in which the words appear are different, but not the way the words themselves appear. No word has changed form. The meaning has changed only by the different arrangement. In Greek the order of the words in the sentence is not as important as the relationship between the words of a sentence. This interaction is shown by changing the endings of words thus revealing the relationship. This change in the endings and forms of a word is known as a declension.

Anér is the word as it is found when it is the subject of a verb (the Nominative case). This is the form presented and first seen in lists of words, lexicons and dictionaries.

The same word *anér* changes into the form *andra* when it is the direct object/recipient of the action of a verb (the Accusative case), etc.

Anér and *Anthròpos*

So, having looked at *anér* in all its forms and comparing it with the use of *anthròpos*, in particular when both are translated in English as 'man', a clear picture arises (see also Appendix 3).

Anér

Strong's lexicon asserts 'a man (properly as an individual male)' – (Strong's Exhaustive Concordance of the Bible including Dictionary of the Greek Testament by James Strong of Abingdon, Nashville: Page 12 of lexicon).

I agree. My research shows *anér* is used to express 'a particular man' whilst *anthròpos* has the emphasis of 'any man, a type of person, someone, etc'.

Anér = a (particular) man or, a husband

Anthròpos = a man (any), a person, someone

Anthròpos is therefore the word Jesus uses when he calls himself '**the Son of Man**' because he is not the son of a particular man, but of mankind. This distinction shows up well in the plural since *anér* will then be used for a particular group of male persons whilst *anthròpos* has the emphasis on 'peoples' including men and women.

A good example

Both words in the same verse in John's gospel can be seen when the feeding of the 5,000 is mentioned:

> . . . And Jesus said, 'Make the men (*anthròpous*) sit down.' Now there was much grass in the place. So the men (*andres*) sat down, in number about five thousand.
>
> *John 6:10 JM*

As soon as the men had been counted in John's mind they then became a particular group of men and he used the word *anér* (in one of it's plural forms). The first occasion it was just 'peoples' in his mind (as translated in NIV, NKJV, et al), so he used *anthròpos*. It would be correct to translate "Make the people sit down".

When we look at the following two passages it will be further seen that the emphasis of 'anér' on its own is 'a particular man':

Blessed is the man to whom the LORD shall not impute sin.

Romans 4:8

Blessed *is* the man who endures temptation . . . *James 1:12*

In both verses, the Greek word for 'man' is *anér*.

What is significant is that the Greek text in these does not contain the definite article 'the' in front of *anér*. This is important as there is an appreciation of the fact that *a particular person* is understood, so that in English, the definite article needs to be added. This is a further indication to us, that by itself (without 'the') *anér* has the emphasis of a particular person.

In 1 Corinthians 11:3, the word for 'man' is *anér*, and it is found with the definite article 'the' in front, which defines 'the noun' as a distinct noun unlike 'a noun' which could be any.

Now, Greek does not have a separate word for the indefinite article 'a, an', so it is added (at will) in translating when there is no definite article presented. We are now ready to see what the following means in 1 Corinthians 11:3,

. . . kephalé-de gunaikos ho anér . . .   *1 Corinthians 11:3*

. . . But head of a woman the [particular] man . . .

We know it is 'of a woman' because the word *guné* is in its genitive form (the case of 'belonging to/offspring of'). In English it is expressed by adding 'of'.

Ephesians 5:23 is a good example showing *gunaikos* and *anér* with the same declensions as 1 Corinthians 11:3

> . . . hoti ho anér estin kephalé tés gunaikos, hòs kai ho Christos kephalé tés ekklésias . . .

> . . . for the husband is head of the wife as also the Christ [is] head of the assembly . . .

So, I ask myself:

Who is the particular man of a woman?

Answer: No one but her own husband.

And since *anér* is the Greek word from which to translate 'husband', to avoid confusion 1 Corinthians 11:3 means:

> . . . and head of a woman the husband . . .
>
> *JM and also translated this way by the Amp.V, GNB1&2, RSV, LB . . .*

This passage therefore does not mention a general headship of man over woman but only of a particular man over a woman: her husband.

It is of note that when Paul said "**the head of every man is Christ**" he does not continue with the head of **every** woman is the husband. Perhaps he was conscious that not every woman is married, but in his day was it not the norm for a woman to be married? Certainly, when he wrote to Timothy about widows he encouraged the younger to remarry thus pointing to such a norm (1 Timothy 5:14). Numbers 30 gives us an indication that in Hebrew homes the head of the house was either the husband or the father of the unmarried woman. A good chapter too to give a pointer to man's unhelpful passivity in that if a woman makes a vow and the man says nothing, then her vow stands. Equally the widow and the divorced woman living on their own stood alone in what they vowed.

> But any vow of a widow or a divorced woman, by which she
> has bound herself, shall stand against her.   *Numbers 30:9*

Just as these women alone stood before God and were responsible thus making the Lord their head, so today the unmarried woman stands with Christ as her head.

1 Corinthians 11:3 cannot be used therefore to understand a general headship of man over woman.

A comparison

Just as the Pharisees legalised and imposed a certain view and practise concerning the Sabbath which Jesus refuted by saying '**The Sabbath was made for man, and not man for the Sabbath**' (Mark 2:27), so also the creation order of woman being made after the man was done for the marriage's sake – as an example to the order of responsibility within it – and not for general functions between the genders.

Which is why we also have the instruction '**Wives submit yourselves to your own husbands**' i.e. not someone else's husband (Ephesians 5:22, Colossians 3:18, 1 Peter 3:1).

The second passage to look in detail now is 1 Timothy 2:12.

13

1 TIMOTHY 2:12

In the previous chapter I mentioned three passages of the New Testament as being the likely candidates for the reasoning of the late John Wimber of Vineyard Christian Fellowships for not having women involved in the top government of the church. We saw how this was likely to consist of passages within 1 Corinthians 11, 1 Corinthians 14 and 1 Timothy 2. I dealt with 1 Corinthians 11 as encapsulated by verse 3 and the reasons were given to show that this was best translated as follows:

> . . . and head of a woman the husband . . .
>
> *1 Corinthians 11:3 JM*
> *As also translated this way by the Amp.V, GNB1&2, RSV, LB*

This accurate rendering removes the passage from use as an indication that there is a general male headship over woman. We are now left with 1 Corinthians 14 and 1 Timothy 2. The verses in detail are 1 Corinthians 14:34 and 1 Timothy 2:12. What are we to make of these passages? Timothy is probably the most used and seemingly clear-cut text to forbid women involvement in church leadership or teaching:

> And I do not permit a woman to teach or to have authority over a man, but to be in silence.   *1 Timothy 2:12*

On it's own this passage seems quite sufficient. Paul does not permit women to teach and further, any exercise of authority over a man is forbidden. Certainly this is what is written in this 'sound byte' of many translations.

Now, a reading of the immediate context and, particularly when this is done directly from the Greek, a number of anomalies show up as divergent with this thinking. These make me question the accuracy of emphasis and meaning given by the immediate appearance mentioned. In the Greek text, verse 11 is not separate from verse 12 but sets the scene for it. Verse 12 is an extension, not a separate command. Verse 11 states:

> Let a woman learn in silence with all submission.
>
> *1 Timothy 2:11*

So what we have is an exhortation not to allow – by Paul's own example '**I do not permit**' – women to teach or bear authority, but only *when* in a learning situation. This is re-emphasised by Paul then by mentioning afresh the attitude '**to be in silence**': in others words the first words of the sentence (in V.11 in the Greek), '**a woman in quietness**' and the last words of the same sentence (in V.12) are '**in quietness.**' Paul is using the same phrase at the beginning and at the end: *en hésuchia* – **in quietness**.

The immediate setting therefore encapsulated at front and end by this phrase shows this is dealing with a public learning situation. And to show these sentences are together both the learning context and the injunction above are sandwiched by the same phrase: Clearly confirming the immediate setting: A woman in quietness/silence . . . but to be in quietness/silence. Here are verses 11-12 in the Greek:

Guné - en - hésuchia - manthanetò - en - pasé – hupotagé.
* didaskein - de - gunaiki (or, gunaiki de didaskein) - ouk -

epitrepò, * oude - authentein - andros, - all' - einai - en - hésuchia.   *1 Timothy 2:11-12*

To help show how this literally translates here follows the two verses in full and please note that dashes are to help follow the direct translation as are the asterisks * (used here at the so-called 'punctuation' breaks of the Greek Text 'used' – N.B. very early extant manuscripts have no space in between words nor punctuations):

(a) woman/wife - in - quietness/silence - learn let (her) - in - all - submissiveness/subjection; * to teach/instruct - but/and – to/for (a) woman/wife - not - I allow/permit, * nor – to have/exercise authority – of (a) man/husband, - but – to be - in - quietness/silence.

In quietness let a woman learn in all submissiveness; and I do not allow for a woman to teach, nor to exercise authority of a husband, but to be in quietness.   *1 Timothy 2:11-12 JM*

Let a woman learn in silence with all submission. And I do not permit a woman to teach or to have authority over a man, but to be in silence.   *1 Timothy 2:11-12 NKJV*

As can be seen there are a few differences between my direct final translation and that of the NKJV. Some of the translation done on 1 Timothy 2:12 has been overlooked or, left undone by the majority of Bible translations (I have looked at 27 to date), there is therefore the need to demonstrate the authenticity of my rendering:

1. Of the versions I have observed only 4 translate the word 'woman/wife' with its dative (the grammatical

125

form of the word showing impersonal/third party interest) [2 French versions, 1 interlinear and the J.B.]: In English this is done by adding 'to' or 'for'. *guné* is the word as the subject of a verb (Nominative Case), in the text it is *gunaiki* the Dative form.

An example of what I mean is Matthew 19:5

Kataleipsei - anthròpos – ton – patera – kai – tén - métera, * kai – proskolléthésetai – té - **gunaiki** - autou,

Matthew 19:5

(he) shall leave – (a) man – the – father – and – the – mother, * and – (he) shall be joined – the – **to/for (a) wife/woman** – of his,

. . . a man shall leave his father and mother and be joined **to** his **wife** . . .   *Matthew 19:5 NKJV*

All I want to show here is that *gunaiki* means 'to a wife/woman' or, 'for a wife/woman'. For more on *guné* I refer the reader to Appendix 2.

2. Only 3 versions translate the word *anér* 'man/husband' in its Genitive form (the grammatical form showing 'genus') and they are all interlinear translations. In English this is done by adding "of" or " 's" to the noun in question. *Andra* is the form of the word as a direct recipient or object of the verb (Accusative Case), in the text it is *andros* the Genitive form. On this part of the translation I wish to spend some time due to the importance to the whole meaning. Here follows the examples of the Genitive simple use of *anér* in the New Testament. There are other uses of the Genitive, but they do not feature here:

Andros

All emphasis added is mine (so the reader can see what he is looking at)

1. . . . who were born, not of blood, nor of the will of the flesh, nor of the will **of man**, but of God. *John 1:13*

   . . . hoi – ouk – ex – haimatòn - oude - ek - thelématos - sarkos - oude - ek - thelématos - **andros** - all' - ek - THeou – egennéthésan.

   . . . the - not - out of/from - bloods - nor - out of/from - will - of flesh - nor - out of/from - will - **of (a) man** - but - out of/from - God - (they) were born.

2. For the woman who has a husband is bound by the law to *her* husband as long as he lives. But if the husband dies, she is released from the law **of** *her* **husband**.

   Romans 7:2

   hé – gar – hupandros – guné – tò – zònti – andri – dedetai – nomò. * ean – de – apothané – ho – anér – katérgétai – apo – tou – nomou – tou – **andros**.

   the – for – married [by a husband] – (a) woman – to the – living – husband – is bound by – law; * if – but – should die – the – husband – she is cleared – from – the – law – of the – **(of a) husband**.

3. But I want you to know that the head **of** every **man** is Christ, the head of woman *is* man, and the head of Christ *is* God. *1 Corinthians 11:3*

   (see the previous chapter for an alternative accurate rendering)

127

THelò –de – humas – eidenai, * hoti – pantos – **andros** – hé – kephalé – ho – CHristos – estin. * kephalé – de – gunaikos – ho – anér. * kephalé –de – CHristou, * ho – THeos.

I wish – but – you – to know, * that – of every – **(of a) man** – the – head – the – Christ – is; * head – but – of a woman – the – husband; * head – but – of Christ, * [the] – God.

4. For a man indeed ought not to cover *his* head, since he is the image and glory of God; but woman is the glory **of man**. *1 Corinthians 11:7*

Anér – men – gar – ouk – opheilei – katakaluptesthai – tén – kephalén, * eikòn – kai – doxa – THeou – huparchòn. * Guné – de – doxa – **andros** – estin.

Man – indeed – for – not – he ought – to have covered – the – head, * image – and – glory – of God – being; * woman – but – glory – **of a husband** – she is;

5. Do not let a widow under sixty years old be taken into the number, *and not unless* she has been the wife **of** one **man** . . . *1 Timothy 5:9*

CHéra – katalegesthò – mé – elatton – etòn – exékonta – gegonuia, * enos – **andros** – guné,

A widow – let be put in the list – not – less – years – sixty – being * of one – **(of a) husband** – (a) wife,

6. . . . for the wrath **of man** does not produce the righteousness of God. *James 1:20*

... orgé – gar – **andros** – dikaiosunév – THeou – ou
– katergazetai.

... wrath – for – **of a man** – righteousness – of God
– not – works out.

The purpose of my display of these is to plainly show that
the normal and basic use of *andros* is to say "of a man/a
man's" or, "of a husband/a husband's".

These are the instances in the New Testament that
andros is found. This is just the word *anér* 'a [particular]
man' or, 'a husband' in the Genitive. These examples refer to
the Genitive use in the singular. The plural form is *andròn*.
The instances given are the simple use of the Genitive which
involves the case of belonging to or being the offspring of.
In English this is done by adding the apostrophe: e.g. a
man's wife or, by adding "of": e.g. of the husband. All other
instances of *andros* and their uses as well as all the instances
in plural are given at the end of the 1st Appendix – *Anér*.

As mentioned my purpose in displaying these examples
is to show the reader the normal use of the Genitive of
anér. *Andros* is correctly translated "of a man" "of a husband"
or, "a man's", "a husband's". In Greek there is no separate
word for the indefinite article 'a' or 'an' so this is added or
omitted purely by inclination. Just as with *guné* the word
for 'a wife' or 'a woman' is like the French *femme* can mean
either 'wife' or 'woman' dependent on context. As we also
saw in the previous chapter, when it is meant for 'a man' the
common use-age reveals it is meant of 'a particular man'
because *anér* is being used and not *anthròpos*. So that you can
now see that my translation of 1 Timothy 2:12 is perfectly
reasonable as follows:

> And I do not allow for a woman to teach, nor to exercise
> authority of a husband, but to be in quietness.
>
> *1 Timothy 2:12 JM*

It is of course important to note also that if I wanted to say 'of a husband', there is no other way for me to do so than by just *andros* in the Greek.

Now, in view of the preceding chapters explaining God's instruction to Eve to submit her desire to her husband to decide about – for her safety from deception – then it makes full sense to translate as "To exercise authority of a husband" from *authentein andros*. Why? Because that is the authority given to the husband in the one flesh relationship and in a learning setting a woman should not exercise that 'teaching' or 'authority' due to the deception factor.

I could translate this as "to exercise authority of a man", but since this means 'a particular man' and, the authority alluded to, I explained refers to the marriage – the one flesh partnership – then, I think it good and accurate to use the word 'husband'. And more importantly, since I have highlighted the authority of a husband from God's words in Genesis 3:16 and why this was so, it makes no sense to translate other than 'husband'.

My reasoning for translating the above as woman is confined to the fact that *guné* (in the Dative case here: *gunaiki*) is the Greek word from which to translate 'wife' and 'woman' and the understanding is that it is the gender as a whole and not individual wives who are susceptible with that kind of deception. Paul speaks of what he allows. It is not about wives, but all women in the assembly during this learning time only. This is not a time Paul allows for women to interact or teach from the floor, but to be in quietness.

Recap

My reasoning for translating the above as husband is confined to the fact that *anér* (in the Genitive case here: *andros*) is the only Greek word from which to translate 'husband'. It is also due to Paul's ensuing reasoning for the statement he has just made. In verses 13-14 Paul lays his reason upon the creation order and the authority of responsibility a husband has been given to him. This authority to rule over (in a certain context) was as a result of the fall initiated by the deception Eve played a part in (Genesis 3:16b) as I explained in the earlier chapters covering this. This is not a general authority to all men over all women, but to a particular man over his wife in the Lord: Which is why Paul also states elsewhere **'wives submit to your own husbands, as to the Lord.'** (Ephesians 5:22) i.e. not to submit to somebody else's husband. The authority is the husband's not any other man. The authority to decide on a matter and to express it from the floor is not allowed by Paul to women.

Remember, the situation he pictures is a public learning situation (he allows and expects women to teach elsewhere: 2 Timothy 1:5, Titus 2:3-4 – see also chapter 17 entitled *Positive Passages*). But in beginning to see Paul's purpose in saying this, let us see where the instruction ties in with his similar injunction in 1 Corinthians 14:34-35,

> Let your women keep silent in the churches, for they are not permitted to speak; but *they are* to be submissive, as the law also says. And if they want to learn something, let them ask their own husbands at home; for it is shameful for women to speak in church. *1 Corinthians 14:34-35*

14
1 Corinthians 14:34

> Let your women keep silent in the churches, for they are not permitted to speak; but *they are* to be submissive, as the law also says. And if they want to learn something, let them ask their own husbands at home; for it is shameful for women to speak in church.   *1 Corinthians 14:34-35*

This is the 3rd of "the three" main passages and the final 'biggy' to deal with. In a sense by covering at length the words within "**as the law also says**" earlier on I have already begun to look at this.

By already covering 1 Timothy 2:12 also it can be seen the immediate similarities. Both cover the same ground. The word to highlight here as in 1 Timothy is "**learn**". It is the time and portion of a public gathering where learning is involved. This is important.

Paul is not saying women are to be silent at all times. He is not advocating they are not to speak at all times of a church gathering. And why can I say that?

Because, Paul had already said what women can do in the meeting. He says explicitly they can pray and prophesy.

> But every woman who prays or prophesies with *her* head uncovered dishonours her head . . .   *1 Corinthians 11:5*

He is not in 1 Corinthians 14:34 contradicting himself, but again referring now to a learning situation. We can see this by his saying 'if they want to learn something . . .'. I think he is alluding to questions arising in the mind of the hearer as opposed to something with which they came to the meeting to share:

> How is it then, brethren? Whenever you come together, each of you has a psalm, has a teaching, has a tongue, has a revelation, has an interpretation. Let all things be done for edification. *1 Corinthians 14:26*

To share in the meeting teaching, revelation and interpretation within an established order is fine, but to respond to something shared or taught is not (see Chapter 17). It is not that wives, let alone women in general, are not able to think for themselves. It is that Paul is acutely aware of the need for order and the God given kind (which is the prime purpose of 1 Corinthians 14). The imbalance resulting from the opposite activity of releasing to discuss there and then (straight away without delay) are open doors to the enemy to influence the church: Due to the deception entry point in the female make up.

I explained in Chapter 6 onwards what Paul was referring to when he said 'as the law also says'. It is the Genesis 3:16 Command by God to Eve to submit her impressions and feelings relating to a matter onwards to her husband to decide about. In this context it relates to doctrine and belief. In this way the enemy cannot gain entry into the lives of folk by the means of new deception. This is not to do with 'old' deception since that would already be around, but it is to do with fresh influences being given room to affect the gathered lives.

When Paul said "**it is shameful for women to speak in church**" it cannot be at all times when he had already spoken about "**every woman who prays or prophesies**". The "**learn**" part is the difference. It is the listening in quietness that is being asked. And it is the reference to the issue of the 1st deception that is being invoked.

In themselves do the passages discussed show up obstructions for a woman to be involved in a church's government or to teach? No, I don't believe so. They do however point to particular roles of responsibility within the marriage relationship and to a difference in the genders which, when taken into account, will enable the full 'giftings' of individuals concerned to be well used to the benefit of the Church and the glory of God.

But let's not forget what the meetings were like in the early church. Not like today's main gatherings. Perhaps more like some informal home groups. Let's take a look.

15

SYNAGOGUES AND MEETINGS

The synagogue meetings = The gatherings of believers

Well, not quite equal to, but I think very similar in a number of practises. This is what I mean by equal; no more. The early Church gathered in homes and places of meeting which resembled in their format to practises of the synagogues of the Jews. Important to the topic of this book is the fact that early church meetings involved much participation by everyone as they desired to. The difference from many of today's regular Christian gatherings is that there was a lack of 'us and them'. Synagogues were not the place of a 'performing elite' with a non participating 'audience', but instead a place where any and all could share in a meeting.

This is shown us by the various mentions of synagogues and what happened within them. This 'norm' was then naturally brought in to the early Church. Believers had their own gatherings both in homes and public places. The way they met is an important context and thus a scene to set and establish for the things Paul writes about women to be understood correctly. It is because of this very interaction practise, naturally and constantly occurring, that Paul gives his instructions in 1 Corinthians 14 and 1 Timothy 2 regarding women behaviour and participation. Because of the normal freedom of interaction he was limiting a learning time with the need for abstinence to react, in particular by women.

Both the Gospel records and the book of Acts give us a picture of the synagogue practises. The Gospels do so in regards to Jesus' time in them and Acts in regards to Paul's travels and witness. In Acts I bring out various things Paul does as recounted by Luke – the writer of Acts – which indicates that this active participation and interaction was the norm in the gatherings of Christian believers.

Capernaum's synagogue

The first time the synagogue in Capernaum is mentioned by name is in Mark's gospel:

> Then they went into Capernaum, and immediately on the Sabbath He entered the synagogue and taught. And they were astonished at His teaching, for He taught them as one having authority, and not as the scribes. Now there was a man in their synagogue with an unclean spirit. And he cried out, saying, "Let *us* alone! What have we to do with You, Jesus of Nazareth? Did You come to destroy us? I know who You are – the Holy One of God!"
>
> But Jesus rebuked him, saying, "Be quiet, and come out of him!"
>
> And when the unclean spirit had convulsed him and cried out with a loud voice, he came out of him. Then they were all amazed, so that they questioned among themselves, saying, "What is this? What new doctrine is this? For with authority He commands even the unclean spirits, and they obey Him." And immediately His fame spread throughout all the region around Galilee.
>
> Now as soon as they had come out of the synagogue, they entered the house of Simon and Andrew, with James and John. *Mark 1:21-29*

It is not so much the activity of the unclean spirit I wish to bring to our attention, since this is not a regular occurrence in most places, but the ability and the freedom that the rest of those present had in the synagogue. As soon as Jesus had His interaction with the spirit involved, the folk exclaimed and were heard clearly in terms of what they said. And by saying '**What new doctrine is this? For with authority He commands even the unclean spirits, and they obey Him**', we see that they had recourse to a certain amount of reasoning among themselves as to what had transpired. All part of the freedoms and practise experienced within the synagogue meeting. The next mention of Capernaum's synagogue is in Luke 4:31-37 and is a parallel record of the above Mark account.

As was quoted already, Simon Peter and Andrew's home was not far, and on another occasion in this same synagogue, John gives a record of interaction which was the normal occurrence of the gatherings. I quote from John's gospel the occasion of one such response to something Jesus had just said:

> The Jews then murmured against Him, because He said, "I am the bread which came down from heaven."
>
> And they said, "Is not this Jesus, the son of Joseph, whose father and mother we know? How is it then that He says, 'I have come down from heaven'?"
>
> Jesus therefore answered and said to them, "Do not murmur among yourselves. No one can come to Me unless the Father who sent Me draws him; and I will raise him up at the last day. It is written in the prophets, '*And they shall all be taught by God.*' Therefore everyone who has heard and learned from the Father comes to Me . . . I am the living

bread which came down from heaven. If anyone eats of this bread, he will live forever; and the bread that I shall give is My flesh, which I shall give for the life of the world."

The Jews therefore quarrelled among themselves, saying, "How can this *Man* give us *His* flesh to eat?"

Then Jesus said to them, "Most assuredly, I say to you, unless you eat the flesh of the Son of Man and drink His blood, you have no life in you . . . He who eats this bread will live forever." These things He said in the synagogue as He taught in Capernaum.   *John 6:41-59*

The last sentence tells us this occurred in the synagogue at Capernaum and it can readily be seen that responses to the main speaker or a teaching was an occurrence of the gathering. This is true of the Capernaum meeting place as well as any other.

Nazareth's synagogue

I will start with the Luke account which clearly mentions this is the synagogue at Nazareth.

Then Jesus returned in the power of the Spirit to Galilee, and news of Him went out through all the surrounding region. And He taught in their synagogues, being glorified by all.

So He came to Nazareth, where He had been brought up. And as His custom was, He went into *the* synagogue on the Sabbath day, and stood up to read. And He was handed the book of the prophet Isaiah. And when He had opened the book, He found the place where it was written:

"The Spirit of the LORD is upon Me, because He has anointed Me to preach the gospel to the poor. He has sent

Me to heal the brokenhearted, to preach deliverance to the captives and recovery of sight to the blind, to set at liberty those who are oppressed, to preach the acceptable year of the LORD."

Then He closed the book, and gave *it* back to the attendant and sat down. And the eyes of all who were in the synagogue were fixed on Him. And he began to say to them, "Today this Scripture is fulfilled in your hearing." So all bore witness to Him, and marvelled at the gracious words which proceeded out of His mouth. And they said, "Is this not Joseph's Son?"

And He said to them, "You will surely say this proverb to Me, 'Physician, heal yourself! Whatever we have heard done in Capernaum, do also here in Your country.'"

Then He said, "Assuredly, I say to you, no prophet is accepted in his own country. But I tell you truly, many widows were in Israel in the days of Elijah, when the heaven was shut up three years and six months, and there was a great famine throughout all the land; but to none of them was Elijah sent except to Zarephath, *in the region* of Sidon, to a woman *who was* a widow. And many lepers were in Israel in the time of Elisha the prophet, and none of them was cleansed except Naaman the Syrian." Then all those in the synagogue, when they heard these things, were filled with wrath, and rose up and thrust Him out of the city; and they led Him to the brow of the hill on which their city was built, that they might throw Him down over the cliff. Then passing through the midst of them, He went His way.

Luke 4:14-30

Immediately someone had finished teaching or speaking in the synagogue there was a time of interaction. Here the reaction involved shock and disbelief that Jesus who had been raised in their midst should have such wisdom and knowledge. This instantly afforded Jesus the opportunity to speak into this common state of heart in regards to prophets and their reception. The synagogue meeting offered room for ongoing explanation and instruction following responses and reactions of those present. This reaction at Nazareth is mentioned in the other gospels also.

> And when He had come to His own country, He taught them in their synagogue, so that they were astonished and said, "Where did this *Man* get this wisdom and *these* mighty works?
>
> Is this not the carpenter's son? Is not His mother called Mary? And His brothers James, Joses, Simon, and Judas? And His sisters, are they not all with us? Where then did this *Man* get all these things?" So they were offended at Him. But Jesus said to them, "A prophet is not without honour except in his own country and in his own house." And He did not do many mighty works there because of their unbelief.   *Matthew 13:54-58*

> And when the Sabbath had come, He began to teach in the synagogue. And many hearing *Him* were astonished, saying, "Where *did* this *Man get* these things? And what wisdom *is* this which is given to Him, that such mighty works are performed by His hands!
>
> Is this not the carpenter, the Son of Mary, and brother of James, Joses, Judas and Simon? And are not His sisters here with us? And they were offended at Him.
>
> But Jesus said to them, "A prophet is not without honour except in his own country, among his own relatives, and in

his own house." Now He could do no mighty work there, except that He laid His hands on a few sick people and healed *them*. And He marvelled because of their unbelief. Then He went about the villages in a circuit, teaching.

Mark 6:2-6

Other synagogues and Jesus

The record we have of Jesus and synagogue gatherings also includes the mention of freedom to pray for others. The control from 'the front' was never such that this was not possible. Nor was it too slack not to allow for public chastening of a practise not deemed fit or correct. There was therefore an active leadership role, but never one that stopped others from sharing and interacting. We can see the stepping in of the synagogue ruler in the 4th quote below as the ruler opposes Jesus' practise of healing on the Sabbath. But, immediately, we also see Jesus' defence against this opposition. Today's church gathering gives little room for such freedom and practise. But it was a regular feature of the synagogue and the early Church meeting place.

Now when He had departed from here, He went into their synagogue.

And behold, there was a man who had a withered hand. And they asked Him, saying, "Is it lawful to heal on the Sabbath?" – that they might accuse Him.

Then He said to them, "What man is there among you who has one sheep, and if it falls into a pit on the Sabbath, will not lay hold of it and lift *it* out?

Of how much more value then is a man than a sheep? Therefore it is lawful to do good on the Sabbath."

> Then He said to the man, "Stretch out your hand." And he stretched *it* out, and it was restored as whole as the other.
>
> *Matthew 12:9-13*

Jesus is seen to practise healing ministry freely in Matthew's gospel. This is repeated in Mark's.

> And He entered the synagogue again, and a man was there who had a withered hand. And they watched Him closely, whether He would heal him on the Sabbath, so that they might accuse Him.
>
> Then He said to the man who had the withered hand, "Step forward."
>
> And He said to them, "Is it lawful on the Sabbath to do good or to do evil, to save life or to kill?" But they kept silent.
>
> So when He had looked around at them with anger, being grieved by the hardness of their hearts, He said to the man, "Stretch out your hand." And he stretched *it* out, and his hand was restored as whole as the other.   *Mark 3:1-5*

Here we see Luke's account and Jesus' use of the time to also speak into the attitude of heart of the scribes and Pharisees.

> Now it happened on another Sabbath, also, that He entered the synagogue and taught. And a man was there whose right hand was withered. And the scribes and Pharisees watched Him closely, whether He would heal on the Sabbath, that they might find an accusation against Him. But He knew their thoughts, and said to the man who had the withered hand, "Arise and stand here." And he arose and stood. Then Jesus said to them, "I will ask you one thing: Is it lawful on

the Sabbath to do good or to do evil, to save life or to destroy *it*?"

And looking around at them all, He said to the man, "Stretch out your hand." And he did so, and his hand was restored as whole as the other. But they were filled with rage, and discussed with one another what they might do to Jesus.

Luke 6:6-11

Here in Luke we see the interaction with the leader of the synagogue as mentioned. This occasion involved the healing of a woman with a spirit of infirmity and who had been this way for eighteen years.

Now He was teaching in one of the synagogues on the Sabbath. And behold, there was a woman who had a spirit of infirmity eighteen years, and was bent over and could in no way raise *herself* up.

But when Jesus saw her, He called *her* to Him and said to her, "Woman, you are loosed from your infirmity." And He laid *His* hands on her, and immediately she was made straight, and glorified God. But the ruler of the synagogue answered with indignation, because Jesus had healed on the Sabbath; and he said to the crowd, "There are six days on which men ought to work; therefore come and be healed on them, and not on the Sabbath day." The Lord then answered him and said, "Hypocrite! Does not each one of you on the Sabbath loose his ox or *his* donkey from the stall, and lead *it* away to water it? So ought not this woman, being a daughter of Abraham, whom Satan has bound -think of it- for eighteen years, be loosed from this bond on the Sabbath?" And when He said these things, all His adversaries were put to shame; and all the multitude

> rejoiced for all the glorious things that were done by Him.
>
> *Luke 13:10-17*

So, it can readily be seen that the synagogue was a place where interaction and responses were practised. Paul found this an invaluable way to spread the good news.

Paul's experience in the synagogues

The first occasion we find Paul speaking in the synagogue about Jesus as the Christ during his missionary journeys is in Antioch in Pisidia (as opposed to the other Antioch in Syria where Paul began his travels).

> But when they departed from Perga, they came to Antioch in Pisidia, and went into the synagogue on the Sabbath day and sat down. And after the reading of the Law and the Prophets, the rulers of the synagogue sent to them, saying, "Men *and* brethren, if you have any word of exhortation for the people, say on."   *Acts 13:14-15*

We can see that travellers could partake and, unplanned – unprepared – speaking was possible and practised in the synagogue. I say unplanned in the sense that this was not in any order of service before the gathering time. Since this practise being prevalent, the visitors – In this case Paul and his party – had already in mind prepared what to share. The next synagogue mentioned in Paul's travels is at Iconium.

> Now it happened in Iconium that they went together to the synagogue of the Jews, and so spoke that a great multitude both of the Jews and of the Greeks believed. But

the unbelieving Jews stirred up the Gentiles and poisoned
their minds against the brethren. Therefore they stayed there
a long time, speaking boldly in the Lord . . .   *Acts 14:1-3*

The laity spectator type 'audience' setting common of today's
church meeting where teaching or preaching is heard, and
everyone else is silent, is found diametrically different to the
setting of the early church meeting: it was wholly uncommon
for a clergy and laity split as evidenced today. Also, leadership
was a team function as I shall amplify upon in the next
chapter. Paul said to Titus to **'appoint elders in every city'**
(Titus 1:5) – at a time when there was only one church or
congregation per city. Active interaction between speaker
and hearers was normal practise. The interaction element is
the most important to consider here. The church gathering
was very much copied from the synagogue model in this
aspect and various verses show up well how interaction in
synagogues was the norm:

> Now when they had passed through Amphipolis and
> Apollonia, they came to Thessalonica, where there was a
> synagogue of the Jews. Then Paul, as his custom was, went
> in to them, and for three Sabbaths reasoned with them
> from the Scriptures, explaining and demonstrating that
> the Christ had to suffer and rise again from the dead, and
> *saying*, "This Jesus whom I preach to you is the Christ."
> And some of them were persuaded; and a great multitude of
> the devout Greeks, and not a few of the leading women,
> joined Paul and Silas . . .   *Acts 17:1-4*

Paul is here described as not only reasoning with his hearers
from the scriptures, but also as explaining and demonstrating.

These are clear words to describe a practise of interaction with the speaker. It can be seen that this reasoning with them was not a distant affair but an active interaction at the time of the gathering by the responses recorded in the different synagogues: '**some of them were persuaded**' (Acts 17:4), '**the next Sabbath. . . came together. . . the Jews. . . contradicting and blaspheming, they opposed the things spoken by Paul**' (Acts 13:44–45) and, from the fact that it occurred with different people in the midst and elsewhere, '**he reasoned in the synagogue with the Jews and with the *Gentile* worshippers, and in the market place daily**' (Acts 17:17).

A normal practise of asking questions and 'saying your bit' as it differed from the (main) speaker/teacher existed within the regular public learning situation. It is within this particular setting that Paul advocated women should be allowed to learn, but not to interact. The closest similar setting to today's church is probably the small house group gathering.

The responses to Paul's teaching were good and bad. On occasion he was vehemently opposed and at other times he commended the hearers for their approach to see if these things are so:

> Then the brethren immediately sent Paul and Silas away by night to Berea. When they arrived, they went into the synagogue of the Jews.
>
> These were more fair-minded than those in Thessalonica, in that they received the word with all readiness, and searched the Scriptures daily *to find out* whether these things were so. Therefore many of them believed, and also not a few of the Greeks, prominent women as well as men. *Acts 17:10-12*

Both words 'reasoning' and 'persuading' are regularly used of the activities permitted and practised in the synagogues.

> And he reasoned in the synagogue every Sabbath, and persuaded both Jews and Greeks.
>
> *Acts 18:4*

At Ephesus

> And he went into the synagogue and spoke boldly for three months, reasoning and persuading concerning the things of the kingdom of God.
>
> *Acts 19:8*

The setting

This then is the setting equally recognised in the ongoing gatherings of the 1st believers, once the synagogue was no longer 'the place of meeting'. When Jews and Christians (whether Jews or Greeks) disagreed in belief, the Christians went on to meet separately and have their own meetings. These meetings afforded the continuing practise of active participation for all who had something of value to impart to the meeting and spontaneous reaction and interaction a regular feature. Corinth is probably the best example we have of this since Paul clearly said of their gatherings,

> How is it then, brethren? Whenever you come together, each of you has a psalm, has a teaching, has a tongue, has a revelation, has an interpretation. Let all things be done for edification.
>
> *1 Corinthians 14:26*

There was freedom and expectation of everyone with something to share to be able to do so, in the Christian meeting. Paul's letter speaks into the need for order, within that freedom and practise. Today's meeting differs significantly in needing freedom to practise such sharing and participation in the first place. But, it can readily be seen that this was the norm back then.

It is in this freedom of participation and interaction that any learning section of the meeting be kept free from interruption and responses from women that Paul then said,

> Let your women keep silent in the churches, for they are not permitted to speak; but *they are* to be submissive, as the law says. And if they want to learn something, let them ask their own husbands at home; for it is shameful for women to speak in church. *1 Corinthians 14:34-35*

It is not to say as I have already shared, that they cannot teach or share or instruct themselves, but in the learning time and only then, they are not to interact and get involved due to the reasons explained in the 'deception chapters'. We know this since Paul fully allowed women to prophesy and pray publicly and more.

> . . . every woman who prays or prophesies with *her* head uncovered dishonours her head. *1 Corinthians 11:5*

A clear statement relating to the freedom to partake in praying and prophesying publicly for women which is in direct contrast to the learning time mentioned when Paul said **"Let your women keep silent . . . for they are not permitted to speak"**. This is also the very context given for the equally clear-cut directive in Timothy:

Let a woman learn in silence with all submission.

1 Timothy 2:11

And all this because the meetings of the day allowed much greater freedom of interaction and participation, but which Paul desired not to see misused in the learning period.

Let's not forget that folk in those days did not live by their watches. The food for dinner was not in a timed oven. The radio, TV, newspaper – indeed anything in print (in 'the West') – did not exist. Time with other people was precious. And meeting times in meetings were not limited by a clock. The orchestrated in today's churches with ready menus and liturgy all laid out was not the norm. Nor was the leadership practises.

16

TEAM LEADERSHIP

In the previous chapter I discussed how the meetings of the first Christians involved much greater freedom and participation by everyone than today. Another important context to appreciate as regards the early church is that there was no one person in charge of the local assembly of believers. It was a team job. Leaders can feel protected by fellow leaders as each looks out to cover the blind spots of the other. The relevance of this in regards to women is that any woman leader operates as part of a team, as men do. In this way any individual person's traits that cause imbalance are countered by the team practise. This is especially true of the deception possibilities due to gender.

In the New Testament there are no examples of churches or gatherings of believers where one leader or one person had greater authority than all other leaders in that group. There are clear indicators that the leadership of all churches was a team effort and, plurality of oversight was not just the norm indeed, but it was unknown anywhere, that there was anything other than team leadership. The immediate, simplest and clear reference for this is Paul's instruction to Titus:

> . . . appoint elders in every city as I commanded you . . .
>
> *Titus 1:5*

It needs to be understood that Paul wrote this at a time when a city was the name for any conurbation, town or village, and that there was only one church per city. No divisions existed between Christians that they did not all gather together in any one locality. Denominations and splits came later in church history.

This is the setting then into which leadership was practised, it was a team deal. The norm was for a group of elders in any locale to oversee the running of the church main gatherings and rule on any matters pertaining to the local body of Christ. The headship of the Church was understood to reside in Jesus, but so was the local headship of the assembly. It is with this in view that Paul declared:

> . . . we have the mind of Christ. *1 Corinthians 2:16*

Believers together who are spiritually minded perceive together the will and mind of Christ. Paul's thinking on this was such that he could not conceive a dispute need ever be taken outside the church.

> Dare any of you, having a matter against another, go to law before the unrighteous [unbelievers], and not before the saints? *1 Corinthians 6:1*

This plurality of oversight with Jesus as head was what I believe Jesus had in mind when he said,

> . . . where two or three are gathered together in My name, I am there in the midst of them. *Matthew 18:20*

And decisions made will have heaven's backing.

> Assuredly, I say to you, whatever you bind on earth will be bound in heaven, and whatever you loose on earth will be

> loosed in heaven. Again I say to you that if two of you agree
> on earth concerning anything that they ask, it will be done
> for them by My Father in heaven.   *Matthew 18:18-19*

Jesus said this immediately after explaining what to do in the matters of dispute between believers. The context involves the church agreeing together in the matter of discipline, because this is the way to discern the mind of Christ. Paul also explicitly advocated this method of disciplining: of making a judgment upon another. We have an example of this in Corinthians and find he clearly states that the punishment or judgment should be decided and carried out when they are gathered together and acting together:

> For I indeed, as absent in body but present in spirit, have
> already judged, as though I were present, *concerning*
> him who has so done this deed. In the name of our Lord
> Jesus Christ, when you are gathered together, along with
> my spirit, with the power of our Lord Jesus Christ, deliver
> such a one . . .   *1 Corinthians 5:3-5*

He later wrote in a subsequent letter that they should now consider restoring this person (2 Corinthians 2:3-11) and affirms that their prior decision was done by '**the majority**' (verse 6).

James

James equally saw a team leadership situation in effect when he said that the sick should call for the elders of the church. These things were part and parcel of the function of elders. Here is the James passage where the elders (in plural) are called upon:

> Is anyone among you sick? Let him call for the elders of the church, and let them pray over him with oil in the name of the Lord.
> *James 5:14*

It can readily be seen that to James it was normal that a church's leadership comprised of a group of elders. This is an example of a team job.

Ephesus

The team at Ephesus can be seen when Paul made his last visit there to say goodbye.

> ... Paul had decided to sail past Ephesus ... From Miletus he sent to Ephesus and called for the elders of the church ... now I know that you all, among whom I have gone preaching the kingdom of God, will see my face no more ... Therefore take heed to yourselves and to all the flock, among which the Holy Spirit has made you overseers, to shepherd the church of God ... *Acts 20:16-28 (context up to verse 38)*

Here we see Paul speaking to the elders of the church. He says they all have been made overseers to the flock of the one church at Ephesus.

Antioch

At Antioch just north of Syria on the coast, Saul spent some time before he was known as Paul. The first mention of him as Paul is in Acts 13:13; prior to that we know him as Saul. We don't have an account of the whole team of leaders at Antioch in Syria, but since we only have talk of a church in any one town or city throughout the New Testament, it is of interest that the group at Antioch also included a team of prophets and teachers.

> Now in the church that was at Antioch there were certain prophets and teachers: Barnabas, Simeon who was called Niger, Lucius of Cyrene, Manaen who had been brought up with Herod the tetrarch, and Saul.   *Acts 13:1*

Saul was recognised as part of the group of teachers and prophets at Antioch. As they fasted and waited on the Lord together God directed them as to the next phase in Saul's ministry and calling. He was now ready to be sent out.

> As they ministered to the Lord and fasted, the Holy Spirit said, "Now separate to Me Barnabas and Saul for the work to which I have called them." Then, having fasted and prayed, and laid hands on them, they sent *them* away.
>
> *Acts 13:2-3*

Although the Greek verb *apostellò* is not being used in this verse, it's basic meaning 'to send out' is understood from then on of the ministry of Saul and Barnabas. They were from that point on known as 'apostles'. The church leadership together heard the Lord and confirmed the call the Spirit had already implanted in the hearts of these men. They were released into it as together the team leadership heard God's will on these things. This is a visual peek into the 5-fold ministries needful to make the local church function effectively with Jesus at the head. The 5-fold ministries Paul mentions in Ephesians 4:11 are there for the church to be fully equipped and function properly and they comprise of apostles, prophets, evangelists, pastors and teachers.

Of course for this to work today dialogue and co-operation needs to occur between all the separated bodies of Christians in any locale.

The practise of team leadership and the regular interaction of the whole body of a church results in life and growth as well as being effective in the noticing of the enemy's activity. Let alone free the individual leader who feels called to more than pastor-ship as time goes by to then be released into what God has been preparing in them.

Heresy and division spotted

Paul wrote:

> For there must also be factions among you, that those who
> are approved may be recognised among you.
>
> *1 Corinthians 11:19*

In the King James this reads,

> For there must be also heresies among you, that they which
> are approved may be made manifest among you.
>
> *1 Corinthians 11:19 KJV*

Now this needs a little unpacking. The Greek word for 'must' here is *dei*, it is incumbent, needful, ought. As opposed to *anagké*, it is obligatory, compulsory (as in Romans 13:5 related to obeying the law of the land). In other words heresies and factions will happen due to the normal course of events with the kingdom of darkness and the kingdom of light in conflict and apparent, in the midst of the local church. The other word to look out for is the Greek word *haireseis,* which is translated above as 'factions' and also 'heresies'. It is of note that to translate heresy as a word from English into the Greek there is no other available. Basically due to the proximity of the Greek to the word for choice, to choose – haireò/haireòmai I think the emphasis is on a choice in the group to divide along the lines of 'a thinking', an idea, a tangent. Heresy is a choice. Paul warned of this possibility to the elders at Ephesus as part of his farewell speech.

> Therefore take heed to yourselves and to all the flock, among which the Holy Spirit has made you overseers, to shepherd the church of God which He purchased with His own blood. For I know this, that after my departure savage wolves will come in among you, not sparing the flock. Also from among yourselves men will rise up, speaking perverse things, to draw away the disciples after themselves. Therefore watch, and remember that for three years I did not cease to warn everyone night and day with tears.
>
> *Acts 20:28-31*

From among the elders themselves would arise this difficulty, let alone from possible newcomers. The enemy in his subtlety makes use of whatever openings he has to divide in his attempts to conquer. By the practise of team leadership and interaction of the body, heresy is spotted by those the Lord approves as Paul's verse in Corinthians tells us. The practise allows the servant of God to speak and be heard. Whether this is a child or a seasoned warrior, the Lord sees the enemy's activity and all who wait on Him have the opportunity to hear and learn in preparation for the enemy's attempts upon the body of believers. A regular response of wisdom and truth imparted into the group by an individual identifies them as approved by the Lord. Especially as these things 'speak into' the error of the hour, for they are a living response in the present warfare occurring. That is my appreciation of the Corinthians passage. Unfortunately, the lack of communication possibilities without team leadership and regular body interaction, in many churches today – as per the synagogue like practise – prevents such a 'hearing' of these things. And therefore prevents in the manner Paul envisaged for some to be recognised as approved of God. Let alone prevents the protection offered by the Lord's input in this way.

But if this were practised, then it could readily be seen that God approves and uses women as well as men to speak regularly into issues. To thus be recognised as approved of God. To be seen as growing into a prophetic ministry or, a leadership role of some kind. Just as Huldah of old or Deborah were recognised in Israel, so also the need exists for this recognition in the church today. Or, like Philip's daughters in the New Testament (Acts 21:8-9). I will now share on positive passages in the next chapter.

17

POSITIVE PASSAGES

Paul says women can teach

> How is it then, brethren? Whenever you come together, each of you has a psalm, has a teaching, has a tongue, has a revelation, has an interpretation. Let all things be done for edification.
>
> *1 Corinthians 14:26*

I wish to start by showing from other uses of the word *brethren* that Paul's use here includes women in his thinking. In other words they are clearly shown in his language (his words) to be free to teach and share revelation, interpretation, etc: indeed Paul says women can teach.

> Therefore, my brethren, when you come together to eat, wait for one another. But if anyone is hungry, let him eat at home, lest you come together for judgment . . .
>
> *1 Corinthians 11:33-34*

Here we see Paul writing to the church at Corinth about communion: The taking of the Lord's Supper together. He is not excluding women or suggesting only men partake, but instead using the term *brethren* generically to say similar to our "Come on folks let's . . ." or, "My friends I appeal to you . . .". He uses the term *brethren* in the same fashion elsewhere.

> Now concerning spiritual *gifts*, brethren, I do not want you to be ignorant . . .
>
> *1 Corinthians 12:1*

Paul did not want anyone whether man or woman to be ignorant about spiritual abilities given by the Holy Spirit. One of the abilities he then lists is prophecy.

> . . . the manifestation of the Spirit is given to each one for the profit *of all* . . . to another prophecy . . .
>
> *1 Corinthians 12:7,10*

So prophecy is one of these manifestations he wishes them to know about. Earlier he had already said:

> . . . every woman who prays or prophesies with *her* head uncovered dishonours her head . . . *1 Corinthians 11:5*

Prophecy is a recognised spiritual 'gift' used by women. Spiritual 'gifts' are to be understood by both men and women. So it is normal to expect Paul's desire for men and women, to know and understand about these activities of the Spirit. His use of the term *brethren* then is generic and inclusive of women. This can thereby be understood of his last use of the term in regards to the topic of 'the gifts':

> Therefore, brethren, desire earnestly to prophesy, and do not forbid to speak with tongues. Let all things be done decently and in order. *1 Corinthians 14:39-40*

The examples of Paul's use of the word 'brethren' this way are numerous. Another good example is Galatians 6:1

> Brethren, if a man is overtaken in any trespass, you who *are* spiritual restore such a one in a spirit of gentleness, considering yourself lest you also be tempted. *Galatians 6:1*

It is of note that in the Greek he does not use *anér* for 'a man' but *anthròpos*: Since using *anér* would mean '(a) [particular] man/(a) husband' as previously highlighted in chapter 12. So it can be seen both in his use of 'brethren' here and *anthròpos* for 'a man' meaning 'someone', that Paul is including women as able to be overtaken in a trespass and able to be 'spiritual' and a help in such situations.

When Paul finishes off a letter too his use of the word brethren is inclusive.

> Finally, my brethren, be strong in the Lord and in the power
> of His might . . . Peace to the brethren, and love with faith,
> from God the Father and the Lord Jesus Christ.
>
> *Ephesians 6:10, 23*

Paul having written to husbands, wives, children, was finishing off with "brethren".

This therefore makes the use of the term *brethren* in the midst of these examples perfectly reasonable to understand in no other way than generic and that women are definitely included:

> How is it then, brethren? Whenever you come together,
> each of you has a psalm, has a teaching, has a tongue, has
> a revelation, has an interpretation. Let all things be done
> for edification. *1 Corinthians 14:26*

Paul is saying therefore that women as well as men when they come to church have occasion to bring a teaching and to thereby teach it to the assembly within the order of the gathering: As is the direction upon men and women: Edification of all and order being Paul's concern.

Paul says obey women

Just as men are to be obeyed so are women who speak the things of God or do the work of the Lord, as recognised by Paul. His warnings in regards to those who deceive and lead people astray are about men as much as women. He never specifies. He just says not to take heed of them. Similarly when he knows someone who is faithful to the Lord he commends them and says their requests should be heeded and here we have a specific example of a woman named as such by Paul.

> I commend to you Phoebe our sister, who is a servant of the church in Cenchrea, that you may receive her in the Lord in a manner worthy of the saints, and assist her in whatever business she has need of you; for indeed she has been a helper of many and of myself also.   *Romans 16:1-2*

It is of note that the word for servant, of the church in Cenchrea, is the Greek *diakonos*. Paul uses the same word for the list of character traits and exemplifying deeds of someone to be picked as a 'deacon' in 1 Timothy 3 (I discuss 1 Timothy 3 a little more in the next chapter). Here Paul is saying that this lady is to be assisted in whatever she says she needs. So, just as Abraham was told by the Lord to obey Sarah his wife in the matter of Isaac and Ishmael (Genesis 21:12), so also in the things spoken from God, women are to be heeded and obeyed: Just as men should be.

There is of course a general instruction from Paul to submit to everyone who works and labours with him or, had done so. In saying that specifically, Paul was therefore including all the women he mentioned as his helpers. This is so in view that he says 'everyone' and not just the men amongst those who work and labour with us.

> I urge you, brethren . . . that you also submit to such, and
> to everyone who works and labours with *us*.
>
> *1 Corinthians 16:15-16*

A few verses later Paul then mentions two very prominent persons who have worked and laboured with him: Aquila and Priscilla.

> The churches of Asia greet you. Aquila and Priscilla greet
> you heartily in the Lord, with the church that is in their
> house.   *1 Corinthians 16:19*

To those in Rome Paul wrote about them as clear fellow workers.

> Greet Priscilla and Aquila, my fellow workers in Christ
> Jesus . . .   *Romans 16:3*

And, of course when they first met we have a good record of their working together.

> After these things Paul departed from Athens and went to
> Corinth. And he found a certain Jew named Aquila, born in
> Pontus, who had recently come from Italy with his wife
> Priscilla (because Claudius had commanded all the Jews to
> depart from Rome); and he came to them. So, because he
> was of the same trade, he stayed with them and worked;
> for by occupation they were tentmakers. And he reasoned
> in the synagogue every Sabbath, and persuaded both Jews
> and Greeks.   *Acts 18:1-4*

So, we find that not only were Aquila and Priscilla fellow workers with Paul, but they were both in the leadership team of the church that met in their house. They are always mentioned together. And it is normal thereby to understand Paul's injunction for the brethren to submit to Priscilla just as much as Aquila in anything appropriate in the Lord. Let's not forget, as discussed in the previous chapter, the norm that local church leadership was always a team function.

Paul says women are to teach

Yes, in general this is so. The specific injunctions when they are told to be quiet, submissive and not to teach only apply to the public learning event. At the other times as we saw, in regards to their bringing a teaching to the assembly as mentioned in the beginning of this chapter, they are free to do so. But, Paul goes on to specify their importance in specific teaching also. Writing to Titus he says:

> But as for you, speak the things which are proper for sound doctrine: that the older men be sober, reverent, temperate, sound in faith, in love, in patience; the older women likewise, that they be reverent in behaviour, not slanderers, not given to much wine, teachers of good things – that they may admonish the young women to love their husbands, to love their children, to be discreet, chaste, homemakers, good, obedient to their own husbands, that the word of God may not be blasphemed.   *Titus 2:1-5*

I thought to give a fuller context of the portion in question. This shows that Paul was clear in requiring men to 'be sober, reverent, temperate, sound in faith, in love, in patience' as much as women to be 'reverent in behaviour, not slanderers, not given to much wine' no gender difference there. But, what is explicit for the older women is that they be encouraged, not discouraged to be 'teachers of good things'. Of course the specific reference Paul makes is to teaching of younger women. It is of note therefore that he is not suggesting men teach here in this area of the life of women. There is a specific gender need here to have women teach women in regards to personal and private matters. If it takes up to a lifetime of appreciating what women go through to enable an older woman to teach a younger one, it is not a general teaching role for any man. One may be called to this, but if specially equipped and trained in particular by the Lord, but this would be the exception and not the rule. As to deception Paul makes no reference here and it is understood that he esteems older women to be able to do this task. Similarly with women he speaks of their teaching of children including younger men and here doctrine is not an issue. He sees no problem of sound dogma be taught by women: Especially to their own children. This is seen by Paul's commendation of the faith of Timothy's grandmother and mother which they held before him. It is understood thereby that they taught Timothy in regards to the faith and Paul fully approved.

> . . . I call to remembrance the genuine faith that is in you, which dwelt first in your grandmother Lois and your mother Eunice, and I am persuaded is in you also.   *2 Timothy 1:5*

We know Timothy was mainly taught by his mother in these things since Paul's first account of his meeting Timothy recounts her qualities in this.

> Then he came to Derbe and Lystra. And behold a certain disciple was there named Timothy, *the* son of a certain

> Jewish woman who believed, but his father *was* Greek. He
> was well spoken of by the brethren at Lystra and Iconium.
>
> *Acts 16:1-2*

And we know that Timothy's mother taught him the Scriptures
since Paul reminded Timothy:

> But *as for* you, continue in the things which you have
> learned and been assured of, knowing from whom you
> have learned *them*, and that from childhood you have
> known the Holy Scriptures, which are able to make you wise
> for salvation through faith which is in Christ Jesus.
>
> *2 Timothy 3:14-15*

We can conclude therefore that women are free and
commended to teach sound doctrine to children and young
men. Indeed there isn't a block on them teaching men at all,
but here is a commendation to the act of teaching one young
man. If it is recognised that women are free and can teach
children, then the question arises for any who would limit it
to children, when does a child become a man?

Indeed, does what he was taught as a child become
invalid the moment he becomes a man? Does that not in
and of itself, point to women as teachers of men being fully
valid?

Paul mentions a woman apostle?

Various writers on this topic have made mentions of Junia
in Paul's final passage in Romans to suggest that here in the
New Testament is an example of a woman apostle.

> Greet Andronicus and Junia, my kinsmen and my fellow
> prisoners, who are of note among the apostles, who also
> were in Christ before me.
> *Romans 16:7*

The emphasis by these writers is that Junia is a female name
and that she is of note, that is to say commendable among
the apostles of whom she is one. This is inconclusive however
and the emphasis can equally be laid that these two persons
– Andronicus and Junia – are noted among the apostles as
note-worthy. This does bring a problem however. For Paul
to make the suggestion that other apostles have Junia and
Andronicus in their sights as commendable, then it follows
that Paul knew this from these apostles and some form
of clear communication with several, if not many of them
had been in place. There is little to no witness to such a
communication between the apostles and Paul. We do have
Paul's meetings with James and Peter mentioned, but nobody
else among the apostles (Galatians 1:19; 2:11). Could it be say,
Peter mentioned these characters as having been discussed by
other apostles and told Paul in one of their meetings? Possible,
but I think unlikely. It remains therefore a contender as a
passage for suggesting that Junia was an apostle – as the
meaning. In any case the basic meaning of the Greek verb
apostellò is 'to send forth' or just 'send' and within that basic
Greek understanding of an apostle, every woman missionary
– as someone sent – has been and is an 'apostle'.

A "negative passage" turned around

In John's letters to the churches from Jesus, in the book of
Revelation, we find an evil woman mentioned.

> Nevertheless I have a few things against you, because you allow that woman Jezebel, who calls herself a prophetess, to teach and beguile My servants to commit sexual immorality and to eat things offered to idols. And I gave her time to repent of her sexual immorality, and she did not repent.
>
> *Revelation 2:20-21*

This lady led men astray and prophesied falsely by teaching lies and deceit. Now, what is of note is that the contention against her is not that she was a leader or teaching men, or even an alleged prophetess, but what she taught. It is the things she promoted which are at issue here. Not the acts of teaching men, leading men or, being a prophetess.

Examples of women leadership

There are a number of examples of godly women involved in leadership in the bible: Both in the Old Testament and in the New.

I have already mentioned Cenchrea and Priscilla. Of particular note to many is Deborah as a leader in the midst of Israel. She is named as one of the Judges and now understood as a Boadicea of her day (Judges 4-5). But, due to the use of Paul's writings by various authors and churches to limit the roles of women let's see what he says about the Old Testament:

> All Scripture *is* given by inspiration of God, and *is* profitable for doctrine, for reproof, for correction, for instruction in righteousness, that the man of God may be complete, thoroughly equipped for every good work.
>
> *2 Timothy 3:16-17*

It is of note that Paul's reference is to the Old Testament. These are the very Scriptures which Timothy's mother had been teaching Timothy, which is the context of this passage. Paul advocates that this section of writings in the bible is full of instruction in doing the right thing: '**instruction in righteousness, that the man of God may be complete, thoroughly equipped for every good work**'. And, what can we find in the Old Testament?

A virtuous wife

Proverbs 31 gives an account of the virtues of a wife who fears the Lord (Verse 30). What is significant for our purpose in this chapter is that she is seen to handle her own finances and manage not only her household, but business dealings as well. The husband is not even considered in the process of her purchasing a field. Also we find her being a teacher of wisdom.

> Who can find a virtuous wife?
>
> . . . The heart of her husband safely trusts her . . .
>
> She considers a field and buys it; from her profits she plants a vineyard.
>
> . . . She opens her mouth with wisdom, and on her tongue is the law of kindness.
>
> . . . Her children rise up and call her blessed; her husband *also*, and he praises her . . .   *Proverbs 31:10-31*

There is a direct link however to the way her husband treats her by loving trust and blessing her. How much more should we love and trust our brothers and sisters who desire to serve, and bless them in their efforts? It is a relationship matter and means that time and importance is to be placed on this interaction in the church just as there should also be in the home. The Church after all is the Family of God and should be a reflection of a warm loving and functioning family.

The queen of Sheba

When Solomon answered the Lord's question in a dream and asked for wisdom he got what he asked for (1 Kings 3:5-15). Then the Lord set up some tough problems which only the wisdom He had given Solomon could answer (1 Kings 3:16-28). This wisdom became known far and wide such that men from everywhere in the known world came to hear of it.

> And men of all nations, from all the kings of the earth who had heard of his wisdom, came to hear the wisdom of Solomon.   *1 Kings 4:34*

However, we only have a record of one monarch who came to visit and see Solomon and his wisdom for herself to test it thoroughly, the queen of Sheba.

> Now when the queen of Sheba heard of the fame of Solomon concerning the name of the LORD, she came to test him with hard questions . . . she spoke with him about all that was in her heart. So Solomon answered all her questions; there was nothing so difficult for the king that he could not explain *it* to her . . . Then she said to the king: "It was a true report which I heard in my own land about your words and your wisdom. However, I did not believe the

words until I came and saw *it* with my own eyes; and indeed the half was not told me. Your wisdom and prosperity exceed the fame of which I had heard."

1 Kings 10:1-7 (onto Verse 13 for the whole story)

Now Paul praises the Bereans in their testing of what he had said to them.

Then the brethren immediately sent Paul and Silas away by night to Berea. When they arrived, they went into the synagogue of the Jews. These were more fair-minded than those in Thessalonica, in that they received the word with all readiness, and searched the Scriptures daily to *find out* whether these things were so. Therefore many of them believed, and also not a few of the Greeks, prominent women as well as men. *Acts 17:10-12*

John also tells us plainly:

Beloved, do not believe every spirit, but test the spirits, whether they are of God; because many false prophets have gone out into the world. *1 John 4:1*

But, it took a woman Sovereign to see for herself the truth of the reports about Solomon: To test him and then give ready praise to God for seeing that these things are so. Not only do we see thereby a wise woman, but one that serves and rules a country well: High praise as a record of her diligence and deeds. As an instruction in righteousness therefore this Kings passage encourages the wise work of women in authority: as rulers of men and teachers of wisdom, the latter of which the queen of Sheba is easily seen to perform by having ready questions prepared for Solomon to answer.

Huldah the prophetess

Paul advocated that it would be possible to notice who was approved of God in the midst of a gathering of believers because of the heresies and disagreements that arose. I mentioned this in the previous chapter in regards to team leadership. Now if, as per the practise of the early Church, gatherings involved the freedom of all to contribute at the appropriate section of an assembly, then as time went by the wisdom of God and the teachings uttered by an individual regularly cannot help but reveal that person, as one who hears the Lord, and as Paul said **'that those who are approved may be recognised among you'** (1 Corinthians 11:19). This can readily be seen as something that occurred in regards to Huldah the prophetess. At an occasion of national crisis we see Josiah, king in the land of Israel, immediately requested that the Lord be enquired as to what to do. The priests in charge at the temple immediately turned to Huldah the prophetess. The whole story is recorded in Kings and Chronicles (2 kings 22:8-20; 2 Chronicles 34:8-28). So the instruction in righteousness here is to have a regular interaction and feedback from those in the assembly and that women are no less able to hear from God, such that a recognised ministry can be ascertained.

18

ODDS AND ENDS

Having highlighted from the beginning the big three passages held as the primary banners to the male leadership issue, I have not addressed several related passages in the New Testament. A book related to women and leadership would be incomplete without a mention of the passage which refers to a head covering, let alone perhaps the passage about 'women bearing children'. Both of these are ongoing portions of texts attached to passages already discussed. The head covering passage is contained in 1 Corinthians 11:4-16 and the 'bearing children' passage is in 1 Timothy 2:15. There is also the list of qualifications Paul gives for someone to be a church leader in 1 Timothy 3.

Just as a good look at the Greek has helped to see what was being said in the portions of texts already covered, so also a closer examination in these will help towards a more coherent view of these odds and ends.

The head-covering

The issue of a head covering or a particular hair do, in terms of what it meant fully, is not my particular aim, but to indeed share some of what this passage reveals and my main purpose is to demonstrate that this practise was not imposed by Paul. Whatever form it really was.

By not imposed, I mean this: It was discussed by Paul with an added appeal to the reader's perceptions of correctness;

not to an idea that this was 'heaven bound' instruction. Although I wish to share various thoughts in regards to the issues in hand on the passage, these will not cover the whole range of topics it raises, and my main thrust will be to leave the reader conscious that the practise, whatever it may or should really be, is not obligatory.

Paul in 1 Corinthians 11 is saying some immoveable foundational things, as well as some cultural things. It is important therefore to highlight which is which, and explain my reasons why I say that. But as stated, mostly I would like to point to Paul's developing argument in the Corinthians 11 passage on a covering so that it may be ascertained that whilst he is solid in the foundations, his thinking about a covering is not wholly imposed upon the reader. The reader is actually left with a choice at the end.

As discussed in Chapter Twelve the passage starts off by Paul saying:

> . . . the head of every man is Christ, the head of woman *is* man, and the head of Christ *is* God.   *1 Corinthians 11:3*

We saw how the middle portion of this verse is correctly translated as,

> . . . and head of a woman the husband . . .
>   *1 Corinthians 11:3 JM and also translated this*
>   *way by the Amp.V, GNB1&2, RSV, LB*

Paul then uses this foundation to launch into a discussion about head covering. He starts by saying,

> Every man praying or prophesying, having *his* head covered, dishonours his head. But every woman who prays

> or prophesies with *her* head uncovered dishonours her head, for that is one and the same as if her head were shaved. For if a woman is not covered, let her also be shorn. But if it is shameful for a woman to be shorn or shaved, let her be covered.
> *1 Corinthians 11:4-6*

As we saw in previous chapters Paul already says things here useful to the issues relating to women's participation in meetings: He says explicitly that women can pray and prophesy in public.

His ongoing discussion does not take issue with this freedom, but how it is carried out.

Verses 4-6 just quoted introduce the head covering issue. He then goes back to some foundational things to re-affirm the position in his thinking of a husband in comparison to his wife. As I begin by highlighting the foundations it is of note Paul affirms that the 'one flesh' relationship is the context in which these things apply in Genesis.

> For a man indeed ought not to cover *his* head, since he is the image and glory of God; but woman is the glory of man. For man is not from woman, but woman from man. Nor was man created for the woman, but woman for the man.
> *1 Corinthians 11:7-9*

To appreciate this properly let's look at the Greek, but before this, I wish to say a few things in regards to headship/covering.

The head covering

Much writing and discussion in regards to the meaning of 'headship' let alone a 'covering' has occurred. As already stated I do not wish to add significantly to this or to make a searching assessment of these various thoughts. I will only make a few comments on this area in passing, but nothing conclusive which can be taken from the form of practise Paul might (or might not) have suggested. Indeed within the passage I think there is nothing very clear as to what form the covering should take. The writings on the issue range from a veil to a different way of putting your hair up. As far as the rest of Scripture is concerned there is no obligation or suggestion for a man or a woman to have a head covering: The sole exception in my reading being the mitre or turban for the high priest to wear (Exodus 28:4; Leviticus 8:9; Zechariah 3:5).

There is a bit more in regards to the practise of shaving one's head. It is seen as part of a vow or a ritual cleansing, a sign of a new beginning or new start. But this practice is applicable to women as well as men as part of the Mosaic Law. For example a woman captured as part of war, if intended to be married and kept as wife by an Israeli soldier, had to shave her hair (and trim her nails) as part of the process of new beginnings (Deuteronomy 21:10-12). The same was to be practised by healed lepers as part of their ceremonial cleansing in the Law, though in their case it was all their hair (Leviticus 14:8). As to vows (Numbers 6), the practise remained and in Acts 21:24 we see Paul and other men having their heads shaved as a part of the Jewish custom under Moses law (although it could be read that the text only refers to the men with Paul shaving their heads). When a Levite was dedicated he also shaved all his hair (Numbers 8:7). A sign of a new beginning – a fresh start: Being holy unto the Lord. Here is the text with Paul being told to go in the temple by the Jerusalem church leaders:

> . . . We have four men who have taken a vow. Take them and be purified with them, and pay their expenses so that they may shave *their* heads, and that all may know that those things of which they were informed concerning you are nothing, but *that* you yourself also walk orderly and keep the law.
>
> *Acts 21:23-24*

This practise of shaving one's head by men when making certain vows under Jewish religious practise raises the following question: Is Paul's mention of a woman shaving her head being a shame because she would then be looking like a man? Or, is it some reference to a pagan practise, namely that shaved women were also recognised as prostitutes from pagan temples? It may appear the whole deed of shaving or covering involves a cultural and historical understanding of particular practises of the day.

What is relevant?

This does not take away from the permanent references not set in culture and these I wish to highlight. Let's look at the Greek of verses 7-9. As we saw the passage reads:

> For a man indeed ought not to cover *his* head, since he is the image and glory of God; but woman is the glory of man. For man is not from woman, but woman from man. Nor was man created for the woman, but woman for the man.
>
> *1 Corinthians 11:7-9*

Anér – men – gar - ouk – opheilei - katakaluptesthai – tén – kephalén, * eikòn – kai – doxa – theou – huparchòn. * guné – de – doxa – andros – estin. * ou – gar – estin – anér – ek – gunaikos, * alla – guné –ex – andros. * kai

179

– gar – ouk – ektisthé – anér – dia – tén – gunaika, * alla
– guné – dia – ton – andra.   *1 Corinthians 11:7-9*

(a) husband/[particular] man – (indeed) – for – not
– (he) ought – to have covered – the - head, * image [lit.
'icon'] – and – glory – of God – being; * (a) wife/woman
– but – glory – of (a) husband/[particular] man – (she)
is; * not – for – (he) is – (a) husband/[particular] man
– out of/from – (a) wife/woman, * but – (a) wife/woman
– out of/from – (a) husband/[particular] man; * and/also
– for – not – was created – a husband/[particular] man
– on account of/due to – the – wife/woman, * but –
(a) wife/woman – on account of/due to – the –
husband/[particular] man;

As shown in Appendix 1 – *Anér* is seen to mean 'a particular
man' when it does not refer to 'a husband' and in plural
'a particular group of men'. There are pointers to men in
general here – see below – as well as pointers to a particular
man and woman, i.e. a husband and wife, but the general
understanding is only relevant as seen through the history of
Adam: the one particular man at the beginning.

Because *anér* is used, when Paul is saying, a woman is
glory of a [particular] man, this can be no other than her
own husband.

Whilst in general, the inference is that a man whether
married or not, is the image and glory of God. This is
interesting since when God created man, Eve was no
separate entity yet, but within Adam (at that stage) and it is
understood by this that women bear the image of God too
(Genesis 1:27). This is further understood when James says
in regards to our use of the tongue:

> With it [the tongue] we bless our God and Father, and
> with it we curse men, who have been made in the similitude
> of God.
> *James 3:9*

He says that when we curse someone we are doing it to someone who is made in the image of God. The word James uses for men here is not *anér*, but *anthròpos* in the plural and as seen in Appendix 3 – *Anthròpos,* this use in general refers to peoples including women. But Paul seems to have something more in mind which separates men from women in this regard. Could this be the element which points to God being called Father in general rather than Mother? We are not told the difference. In physical terms all men have both X and Y chromosomes, while women have only two X chromosomes, so every physical cell in the body tells a man he is and a woman that she is. So that Jesus' birth from Mary is really a miracle in that no Y chromosomes came from her. And, we know Jesus is,

> . . . the image of the invisible God, the firstborn over all
> creation.
> *Colossians 1:15*

So Paul wishing to differentiate between men and women says something about men being more a representation of God. What, he does not specify, nor can we. But in saying a woman is the glory of their husband, there is a possible pointer to a marriage issue. The next verse is what may help clarify what is at stake. However before I continue there, it is clear Paul makes a case for man's pre-eminence (in some way) by saying she was made after man, from man and, for man. But, since again this is throughout making use of the word *anér*, it is the particular man that is being seen and not men in general when applied to the glory and the purpose of woman's creation. You cannot stretch the passage to suggest a woman is for any or all men or, that she may be the glory of any other than her particular man. After all she was only after one man and from one man; not all: only Adam qualifies here. Now this brings me one separate thought which demonstrates our passage cannot refer to a general headship of men over women: a denouncement of a two class system. It is simple and effective and is supported by Peter clearly as well as Paul.

Submission of woman

Headship and submission is never a general issue of men over women since all the explicit submissive passages emphasise that women are to be submissive *to their own* husbands. This carries with it the full understanding and appreciation that this means they do not submit to another woman's husband.

> Wives, submit to your own husbands, as to the Lord.
>
> *Ephesians 5:22*
> *See also Colossians 3:18 and 1 Peter 3:1*

Not forgetting, in regards to submission we are all, as believers, to be subject to one another in the Lord, and that particular honour should be given to those who labour for us and on our behalf (Ephesians 5:21; Hebrews 13:17). And Jesus said those who lead are those who serve (Matthew 23:11).

The only time the submission is mentioned in regards to women other than in the marriage context involves the public learning situation: and these we have each in turn covered in previous chapters. This in my view and explanation is only due to the capacity of women to perceive things in a manner that enables deception to be a factor to influence an assembly. But, since this is only relevant in the context of interaction with all present who could speak up and that, always it is seen, is the fact that this was a learning time, then there is no general submission of women to men. There is therefore no suggestion that the woman of God be not part of a leadership team which is – it must not be forgotten – the only form of leadership pictured in the local assembly in the New Testament. Let alone any restriction on teaching, public instruction or preaching upon any matter prepared beforehand.

> . . . women are to be submissive to their own husbands. This carries with it the full understanding and appreciation that this means they do not submit to another woman's husband.

So, in the recognition of Adam's personal need we find that within the one flesh relationship woman was made for him, from him and after him. A wife is the man's glory.

But, are all married? What of the woman who is unmarried? Did not Paul also state that it is good not to marry when he recommended celibacy in certain contexts? Yes, he did.

Are all to marry?

Paul writes clearly about this earlier in the letter to the Corinthians:

> . . . because of sexual immorality, let each man have his own wife, and let each woman have her own husband . . .

> But I say this as a concession, not as a commandment. For
> I wish that all men were even as I myself. But each one has
> his own gift from God, one in this manner and another in
> that. But I say to the unmarried and to the widows: It is
> good for them if they remain even as I am . . .
>
> *1 Corinthians 7:2, 6-8*

Since Paul is also an encourager for folk to dedicate themselves
to God and serve Him without marriage, then it follows he
did not mean the head covering was just an issue of a man
and his wife. It is of note that the word 'men' when he says
'**I wish that all men were even as I myself**' is *anthròpos* and
he is saying this therefore to men and women. So this next
verse is less about the issue of marriage and the feelings men
and women have for each other, but something altogether
different.

So here headship and covering then also takes a 'general'
meaning. And this is shown us by the next verse in our
passage. But here what is most significant, is his declaration
and his overall reason for bringing the subject up in the first
place.

> For this reason the woman ought to have *a symbol* of
> authority on *her* head, because of the angels.
>
> *1 Corinthians 11:10*

This is a central portion of this passage on head-coverings.
Not only is Paul saying this is the reason for all this, but
he begins thereafter to reduce his earlier seemingly emphatic
desire to see it implemented. So this whole passage turns on
this verse in terms of the why? And in terms of how absolute
Paul is about this. Let's look at the Greek:

... dia – touto – opheilei – hé – guné – exousian – echein
– epi – tés – kephalés, * dia – tous - angelous.

1 Corinthians 11:10

... on account of/due to – this – ought – the – woman
– authority – to have – upon – the - head, * on account
of/due to – the – angels;   *1 Corinthians 11:10*

It is a shame that this is all Paul says explicitly here about this reason: '**on account of the angels**'.

But, we have pointers elsewhere as we have already seen earlier in this book. Deception and the influence of the enemy – fallen angels – is the single most core issue Paul has in mind in relation to the order of what goes on in meetings relating to women. This I have discussed at length. I do not see this as a reference to sexual or marital status, since Paul had expressed women's freedom to serve God as much as men in regards to celibacy. But instead I believe Paul is saying that a woman's wearing of a covering is a further pointer, by the woman in the assembly, who practises her freedom to pray or prophesy publicly (for that is what Paul began to address and express as the context), to being aware of the responsibility of the man in her life in these matters: The responsibility of authority related to the influence of angels: As I mentioned and discussed the reason God gives for the woman to submit her fresh overwhelming desires unto her husband. This understanding would agree with the translation in regards to 1 Timothy 2:12 i.e. the authority of a husband: which is to rule in regards to immediate assertions and feelings gained in reaction to an influence in the meeting time. The problem then arises as to what happens about the woman deceived who is not married? We are not told explicitly, but it is inferred by the silence and Paul's ongoing comments that he is not suggesting a male domination in general. We can see this as Paul is then *at pains* to not overextend an idea of male domination by the ensuing verses.

> Nevertheless, neither *is* man independent of woman, nor woman independent of man, in the Lord. For as the woman *was* from the man, even so the man also *is* through the woman; but all things are from God.
>
> *1 Corinthians 11:11-12*

Here we see Paul 'back tracking' of sorts or, more properly, balancing the words he used to show a type of male pre-eminence by saying that even man cannot do it alone. He is not independent of woman just as woman is not independent of man, but all things here need to be in the Lord. With the mind of Christ together, discernment and proper practise can be ascertained. Male lordship is therefore not Paul's agenda; it is the balanced order of things done in the assembly. This means therefore in the case of individuals who share and contribute publicly there is a submission to all in the Lord. Paul is careful then on, not to reiterate or make a hard and fast rule of a 'covering practise', but instead appeals to what the reader can appreciate. He had already said:

> For this reason the woman ought to have *a symbol of* authority on *her* head . . .   *1 Corinthians 11:10*

Ought the woman

Paul says the woman 'ought to', he does not say this is an obligatory thing and she 'must' do this without fail. This is an important point and is borne by his ongoing words appealing to his readers rather than imposing this thinking. It is unlike his instruction in Romans as regards the government and civil authorities.

> Therefore *you* must be subject, not only because of wrath
> but also for conscience' sake.   *Romans 13:5*

Paul for 'must' here in Romans uses the word *anagké*, it is compulsory, it is obligatory. He does not use the more common *dei*, 'it is incumbent', 'you ought to', etc. Here in Romans he is not allowing for any doubt that the law of the land and the authorities are not an option, there is no choice, but obedience in general for the Christian.

So whilst Paul is making a case for woman to have a head-covering he is not imposing it strictly, but says she 'ought to'. The Greek here for 'ought' is *opheilò*: (she) ought – (she) owes – (is indebted) to the reason given. Not forgetting that any wearing of a covering is of no relevance if the wearer is in no way submissive to the mind of Christ in the assembly. It then becomes no different a practise then when Paul decried circumcision as being useless when the heart of the person is wholly uncircumcised: wicked and evil (Galatians 6:12-13). Though to be fair we cannot tell if someone is circumcised by looking at them in the church gathering (being clothed). The point of principle is that wearing something on one's head or having a certain hair do or what clothes we wear is no guarantee of our attitude or submissive heart to the corporal 'mind of Christ'.

It is also to be recognised that the recognition by the mind of Christ in the assembly includes the women as well as the men. It is the recognition of the spirit that speaks which is at issue. Which spirit is someone speaking by? What is the influence or wisdom that brings forth the words uttered?

Judge among yourselves

Paul then ends his subject of a head covering with an appeal; not a command.

> Judge among yourselves. Is it proper for a woman to pray to God with her head uncovered? Does not even nature itself teach you that if a man has long hair, it is a dishonour to him? But if a woman has long hair, it is a glory to her; for *her* hair is given to her for a covering. But if anyone seems to be contentious, we have no such custom, nor *do* the churches of God.   *1 Corinthians 11:13-16*

Bringing back the whole issue to what women do publicly when they speak in contribution, Paul concludes with an appeal to the readers to judge for themselves. Can women do this without a head covering? Can they do this with short hair or shaved? Is it not better for women to have long hair? You decide.

Finally are you contentious?

The word for contentious means a lover of strife: A lover of states of conflict. Paul by this last sentence points to contention on this subject either way is not to be engaged in. It is as if Paul in closing says "Therefore in view of my appeals to your own judgments I am not imposing this line of thought, but recommending it. You are in no way to make it an issue of division or conflict in your midst."

In these words Paul is saying to not fight about this. To impose a rule about this is to force another into a mould not necessarily of their choosing. So Paul's finale is, you decide, but do not fight about it, it is not to be imposed.

1 Timothy 2:15

Now, to the 'bearing children' passage: a passage which has caused difficulties for some. A friend of mine having worked in Romania, since its post President Ceaucescu opportunities, has reported to me that he has heard many to believe that unless women have children they will not be saved. This passage is used to say that.

> Nevertheless she will be saved in childbearing if they continue in faith, love, and holiness, with self-control.
>
> *1 Timothy 2:15*

Immediately this is read, the question arises as to what this is written after? So let us remind ourselves of the context:

> Let a woman learn in silence with all submission. And I do not permit a woman to teach or to have authority over a man, but to be in silence. For Adam was formed first, then Eve. And Adam was not deceived, but the woman being deceived, fell into transgression. Nevertheless she will be saved in childbearing if they continue in faith, love, and holiness, with self-control.
>
> *1 Timothy 2:11-15*

This is more revealing. A command to permit the learning of women is given with a clear restriction as to how this learning takes place. This restriction is explained in turns of the female make up and the order of the Creation, but primarily in terms of the deception possibilities. This restriction explanation then given, Paul tells us that a woman will nevertheless be saved due to a number of factors.

Now, the preceding section to verse 15 has been explained in full in chapter 13. And it was explained in detail by using the Greek and analysing the translation. Equally this verse makes more sense if we do the same here.

> sòthésetai – de – dia – tés – teknogonias, * ean – meinòsin – en – pistei – kai – agapé – kai – hagiasmò – meta – sòphrosunés. *1 Timothy 2:15*

> She shall be saved – but – through – the – childbearing, * if – they abide – in – faith – and – love – and – holiness – with – self-control/sobriety. *1 Timothy 2:15*

This makes more sense to me. Bearing in mind that Paul has just been thinking and sharing his thoughts based wholly on what happened in Genesis his ongoing remark is not distanced from that. God said to the serpent what was to occur in regards to the woman's Seed and the serpent.

> . . . I will put enmity between you and the woman, and between your seed and her Seed; He shall bruise your head, and you shall bruise His heel. *Genesis 3:15*

We know that Jesus is the only one on biblical record as born of a woman who was a virgin (Matthew 1:23). Jesus is thereby understood as the woman's Seed: Which is also why the capital letter is used by translators. It is further understood that by His sacrifice on the cross Jesus bruised Satan's head permanently. We know Satan is the serpent of old from Revelation 12:9,

> . . . the great dragon was cast out, that serpent of old, called the Devil and Satan, who deceives the whole world . . .
> *Revelation 12:9*

And we know that what Jesus did on the cross severely – permanently handicapped – (bruised the serpent's head) the enemy, since Paul tells us:

> . . . He [Jesus] has taken it out of the way, having nailed it to the cross. Having disarmed principalities and powers, He made a public spectacle of them, triumphing over them in it.
> *Colossians 2:14-15*

So that when Paul says, '**She shall be saved – but – through – the – childbearing**', we can understand this to refer to only one child bearing: That of Jesus 'the' Child who was born of a virgin. The emphasis made by Paul in using the definite article and the fact that childbearing is in the singular makes me read this as involving a single incident. But, Paul goes on in this sentence for fear that having said women will be saved, this is understood as a blank cheque: as if it could be read all women will be saved. He therefore outlines the kind of fruit which identify a believing woman:

> . . . if they continue in faith, love, and holiness, with self-control.
> *1 Timothy 2:15*

Which is basically how I read this verse: Paul had been concentrating on women's behaviour in a public gathering and particularly, the set aside time to learn, he then finishes that instruction showing the importance of the state of heart of a believing woman, encouraging as an aside that they will be saved due to The Child borne by Woman.

The Elders qualifications – an aside from
team leadership in 1 Timothy 3

When Paul wrote to Timothy he included a list of qualifying statements in regards to choosing an overseer or, an official servant. These are the characteristics he sees as befitting an elder, a leader, a recognised helper in the rule and service of the local church, irrespective of the actual names they are actually given by whatever tradition since then: Whether they are today called bishops, elders, pastors, episcopate or, whatever. The following as throughout this book, unless otherwise stated, is from the New King James Version.

> This *is* a faithful saying: If a man desires the position of a bishop, he desires a good work. A bishop then must be blameless, the husband of one wife, temperate, sober-minded, of good behaviour, hospitable, able to teach; not given to wine, not violent, not greedy for money, but gentle, not quarrelsome, not covetous; one who rules his own house well. Having *his* children in submission with all reverence (for if a man does not know how to rule his own house, how will he take care of the church of God?); not a novice, lest being puffed up with pride he fall into the *same* condemnation as the devil. Moreover he must have a good testimony among those who are outside, lest he fall into reproach and the snare of the devil. *1 Timothy 3:1-6*

Paul then gives a similar list for the helpers or deacons in the following six verses. What is immediately noticeable is the references to 'man' from the beginning and onwards as in the words '**if a man does not know how**', let alone the pronoun 'he' and 'his' as in '**he desires a good work**' and '**rules his own house**', etc. This colours the text with the pre-supposition that Paul was excluding women in his thinking. With this in mind, let us look at the Greek of these segments.

> . . . If a man desires the position . . . he desires a good work . . . one who rules his own house well . . . *his* children in submission . . . for if a man does not know how to rule his own house, how will he take care . . . he fall into the same . . . he must have a good testimony . . . lest he fall into . . .
>
> *1 Timothy 3:1-6*

These are seeming pointers to male exclusivity. So, in looking at the Greek the following words are what we need to see to confirm an idea of male leadership:

For 'he':	*autos*
For 'his':	*autou*
For 'him':	*auton*
For 'man':	*anér* or, *anthròpos*

> . . . ei tis episkotés oregetai . . . kalou ergou epithumei . . . tou idiou oikou kalòs proistamenon . . . tekna echonta en hupotagé . . . ei de tis tou idiou oikou prosténai ouk oiden, pòs ekklésias THeou epimelésetai . . . eis krima empesé . . . dei de auton kai marturian kalén echein . . . hina mé eis oneidismon empesé . . .
>
> *1 Timothy 3:1-6*

Which literally gives:

> . . . if any overseer-ship stretches forward to . . . of good a work (he/she) is desirous . . . his/her own house well ruling . . . children having in subjection . . . but if one his/her own house to rule (he/she) knows not, how assembly of God shall (he/she) take care of . . . into crime (he/she) may fall

> ... But it behoves him also a good testimony to have ... lest
> into reproach (he/she) may fall ...   *1 Timothy 3:1-6*

Rather than give numbers next to each section of the English translation, the Greek and the literal rendering which causes back and forth examination, I thought to give the above in a comparative format to enable quick recognition of the relevant portions:

Verse 1 (a)
... If a man desires the position of a bishop ° ei – tis – episkotés - oregetai ° if – any – overseership - stretches forward to ...

Verse 1 (b)
... he desires a good work ° kalou ergou epithumei ° (of) good/well - (of) a work - (he/she/it) is desirous ...

Verse 4 (a)
... one who rules his own house well ° tou idiou - oikou - kalòs - proistamenon ° his/her own – house - well/good - ruling ...

Verse 4 (b)
... *his* children in submission ° tekna - echonta - en - hupotagé ° children – having - in - subjection ...

Verse 5
... for if a man does not know how to rule his own house, how will he take care

° ei – de - tis - tou idiou - oikou - prosténai - ouk - oiden, * pòs – ekklésias - THeou - epimelésetai

° if – but - one - his/her own - house - to rule – not - (he/she) knows, * how - assembly - of God - shall (he/she) take care of ...

Verse 6

... he fall into the *same* ° eis – krima - empesé ° into - crime - (he/she) may fall ...

Verse 7 (a)

... he must have a good testimony ° dei - de – auton – kai - marturian – kalén - echein ° behoves – but - him – also/and – (a) testimony - good - to have ...

Verse 7 (b)

... lest he fall into ° hina mé - eis – oneidismon - empesé ° lest - into – reproach - (he/she) may fall ...

Result

The specific words for 'man', 'he' or 'his' are not to be found anywhere in the Greek. Instead the verbs without pronouns are given and have equal weight of emphasis for either gender.

The sole exception is in Verse 7 (a) where the word *auton* meaning 'him' is found. Since there is no pronoun for 'both an individual woman or man to be used' to mean either/or at the same time, and the general lack of particular male pronouns in the text, I understand this exception as meant in a generic sense: Just as Paul often used the word for 'brethren' to mean 'brothers and sisters' together which I demonstrate in the previous chapter.

Is this a bad translation then?

Well, it all depends on your point of view. Translators operate under a set of rules or basic themes. If, for example the understanding is to give a readable translation with little break up in the flow, then to translate the above like 'he or she desires a good work' and likewise every time a verb is found, then the flow is hindered drastically. In this understanding the translation is good.

If the aim of the reader however is to ascertain doctrine and dogma then, he or she is not helped and there is thereby little alternative then to learn the Greek or, read alternative renderings of a passage or theology based on the text: Hence I trust this section helps here on the matter.

Not least Paul's mention of a man as a possible 'husband' warrants the translator the favoured option to give a male slant. So let's take a look.

What about being a husband?

In this passage there is also a set of words which are not a translation divergence, but a clear possible allusion to male exclusivity. They are:

> . . . A bishop then must be . . . the husband of one wife . . .
> *1 Timothy 3:2*

If Paul meant leadership to be male surely this is shown by the fact that only a man can be a husband? Well, not quite because along with that thinking we would then have to say this man in order to be in leadership needs to have had children: Let alone, a job in a secular environment in order to gain approval from those '**who are outside**', or some other involvement seen and appreciated by non-believers.

We know that Paul did not require marriage prior to leadership from his advice in regards to celibacy. Paul in an unmarried state and discussing matrimony said:

... I wish that all men were even as I myself. But each one has his own gift from God, one in this manner and another in that. But I say to the unmarried and to the widows: It is good for them if they remain even as I am ...

1 Corinthians 7:7-8

Now, if Paul advised his preference that folk remain unmarried, then it follows that he did not suggest that to be a leader you had to be married. To the contrary, his writing to Timothy is about the fact that if you are married, then let that marriage be an example to others. If you have children, let that family order and harmony be an example to others. If you have been involved in secular work, let that be a testimony to your character. So, it is the practises of the person and their character that the passage addresses and not the gender. It is not a call to male leadership. But, Paul does call for team leadership.

19

CAN WOMEN TEACH?
A SUMMARY

We are told by Paul:

> . . . I do not permit a woman to teach . . .   *1 Timothy 2:12*

Moreover he also said,

> Let your women keep silent in the churches, for they are not
> permitted to speak . . .   *1 Corinthians 14:34*

Well, my answer to the Title question is, "Yes."
  The same is true for women being able to speak, "Yes."
How can I say that in the light of these quoted passages?
Because Paul also said,

> . . . the older women . . . be . . . teachers of good things
> – that they admonish the young women . . .   *Titus 2:3-4*

And he commended the teaching work of Timothy's mother
and grandmother:

> . . . I call to remembrance the genuine faith that is in
> you, which dwelt first in your grandmother Lois and your
> mother Eunice . . .   *2 Timothy 1:5*

So, since Paul's first quoted passages are not alone on the issue
of women teaching and he is indeed explicit and implicit

about women teaching elsewhere, it follows that women can teach.

The new question therefore is why did he say women should not in those first passages?

Let alone speak?

Well, let's deal with the speaking first. Is Paul advocating complete silence throughout a church gathering for women?

No.

He also said earlier in the First Corinthians Letter,

> . . . every woman who prays or prophesies with *her* head uncovered dishonors her head . . . *1 Corinthians 11:5*

Leaving aside the issue of a head covering momentarily (as per the previous chapter), Paul is discussing the activity of men and women in a church gathering and by saying how a woman is to do something he is stating that the activity itself is normal practise for women. The activity of praying or prophesying in a public gathering is normal for women as much as men. How they do it was his only immediate concern.

So we can see that Paul does not say that women cannot teach, nor that they cannot speak.

What is special about the 1 Corinthians 14 and the 1 Timothy 2 passages that make them different from the other times Paul mentions the activity of women is that these are public learning events. The setting for these events was significantly different in New Testament times than today. The model followed for the first church gatherings is that of the synagogue. This was a place where everyone can interact, dispute, challenge and contribute during many a learning time. Jesus and Paul having opened the door to women's inclusion in gatherings of believers, Paul is pointing out that the learning time is not one to permit women to interrupt, but to learn in quietness. And Paul in saying this is differentiating between men and women in regards to how they respond to new input.

In today's church it is rare that interaction is freely permitted except perhaps in an informal small group setting. The relevance of not speaking or not teaching is obliterated by that fact. Irrespective of the particular reasoning Paul gives for women not to in the public learning time of his day.

The question remains however why does he say that to women during the public learning time of the gatherings?

The answer lies in the area of deception. More particularly fresh deception arising out of reaction to teaching input. So that the assembly, not being disturbed by immediate responses can all learn what is being taught.

How can I say all this?

Well, when he made those mentions not to teach nor to speak he also said,

> Let your women keep silent in the churches, for they are not permitted to speak; but *they are* to be submissive, as the law also says. And if they want to learn something, let them ask their own husbands at home; for it is shameful for women to speak in church.   *1 Corinthians 14:34-35*

Straight away we see this is a reference to a learning time. Also we see reference made to an understood submissiveness which is also brought into play in the 1 timothy 2 Passage. If only this understanding had not been mislaid, then so much confusion would have been avoided in this matter – in this topic of significance. We are not helped however by a translation error of the 1 Timothy 2 portion. Let's see it now in the NKJV showing well the public learning time and a reference to deception linked to Paul's thinking:

> Let a woman learn in silence with all submission.
>
> And I do not permit a woman to teach or to have authority over a man, but to be in silence.
>
> For Adam was formed first, then Eve. And Adam was not deceived, but the woman being deceived, fell into transgression. *1 Timothy 2:11-14*

Please note Paul makes no reference as to the teacher here being a man or woman. The translation error is in Verse 12: **'And I do not permit a woman to teach or to have authority over a man, but to be in silence'**. My study of the Greek shows that instead of, **'to have authority over a man'**, this should read: **'to exercise authority of a husband'**. In chapter 13 I gave an exhaustive look at the translation of the Greek word *anér*, in the Genitive *andros*, and demonstrate this fully.

The two passages refer to events in the beginning. By saying, **'as the law also says'**, in 1 Corinthians I mentioned that this is a reference to Genesis 3:16 which Paul is also highlighting in the Timothy passage. The whole area of deception as it relates to gender is at issue here as well as to what the Lord has brought into play to cater for the situation as it is, so that all are protected.

The authority of a husband is in ruling over the situations submitted to him. By extension this practise involves deciding over issues discussed or taught. Limits are in place in regards to this authority in that the public learning time where interaction occurs is in view. No more.

In the beginning when Eve was deceived and ate, God's words to her afterwards expressed to her the need to submit her desires for her husband to rule over. This new practise was then a means of protection from being taken in by a desire. This provided a decision gap between the desire and any possible ensuing act. The husband's responsibility is in being active in recognising the truth of the matter and communicating that. This is the authority Paul mentioned a woman not to exercise during a public learning time, but to be in quietness.

Teaching is encouraged at other times.

20

CAN WOMEN GOVERN? A SUMMARY

If women cannot teach and must be silent, let alone submissive, then there is no way that they can govern. But, we have seen they can teach, they can speak, and outside a setting where learning is involved, submission is the same as applicable to men. All believers are under obligation to play their part in terms of decency and order of a public meeting.

> Let all things be done decently and in order.
>
> *1 Corinthians 14:40*

And, all believers are to be submissive to one another.

> . . . Yes, all of *you* be submissive to one another, and be clothed with humility, for *"God resists the proud, But gives grace to the humble."*   *1 Peter 5:5*

This is applicable to leaders, to followers, to women, to men, to young, to old, to all.

So, what is there to suggest women cannot govern?

The creation order has been used to point to a general headship of man over woman.

However we have seen how outside of a learning event the only place where this order matters is in the one flesh relationship – marriage.

The creation order

It is significant that for Paul and indeed for all the apostles, there is no doubt of the reality of this event as per Paul's expressions: a man, Adam, was created and then a woman, Eve was formed after, for and complimentary to him.

> For man is not from woman, but woman from man. Nor was man created for the woman, but woman for the man.
>
> *1 Corinthians 11:8-9*

By this I mean that the creation, let alone the order of creation, is wholly understood as a reality by the writers of the New Testament. As such the order of woman being made after man has a relevance to teaching on behaviour and roles of the two separate sexes. But, this is to be confined to the marriage, the one flesh relationship, in its outworking. Paul made clear that the headship is explicit for the husband and wife, not as a general superiority of one gender over the other.

> For the husband is head of the wife . . .   *Ephesians 5:23*

This I showed by the Greek is what Paul indicated in 1 Corinthians 11:3 within Chapter 12 of this book. The headship issue when related to gender is not to be expressed outside of the marriage situation. Indeed Paul goes on in 1 Corinthians 11 to state:

> Nevertheless, neither *is* man independent of woman, nor woman independent of man, in the Lord. For as the woman *was* from the man, even so the man also *is* through the woman; but all things are from God.
>
> *1 Corinthians 11:11-12*

He was not advocating an expression of headship beyond the marriage relationship.

So for wives, submissiveness to their own husbands is taught, not someone else's husband.

> . . . wives, *be* submissive to your own husbands . . .
>
> *1 Peter 3:1 Ephesians 5:22; Colossians 3:18*

Therefore the creation order does not inhibit a woman to govern.

Finally

In a sense this chapter is just a continuation of the previous one *Can women teach?*

The three main passages which have been stumbling blocks and hindrances to permit women to lead in churches have been looked in detail earlier in this book and summarised by these last two chapters. Let's now conclude things.

21

FINALLY

Finally the issue of women in leadership in the church is satisfied. An understanding and full answer to the blockages as seen in 'the 3 New Testament passages' has been given. The attention is now to be restored to the work of the Divider of unity among the saints – Satan. Deception's challenge is to be met within the practise of the church for it to remain effective: Practises that relate to how leadership carries out its functions and with the provision of effective checks and balances; Practises that relate to how meetings are run allowing participation, but with effective opportunity for discernment. Indeed as has been said by many, the price of peace is eternal vigilance. But peace is not just an absence of conflict, but a harmonious function of activity where all play their part within the local Kingdom economy. This cannot occur if the enemy's regular activity of accusing the Lord's servants and the feeding of false dogma is not nipped in the bud by proper practise.

So what is this book about?

The state of play is that thousands of bible believing churches will not have women in leadership because of seeing verses suggest this should not be. It was good for many of these believers to see that the injunctions in these passages were not related to culture or history, but gender only. It is no longer acceptable to restrict the gender when the root issue of deception is fully catered for: fully recognised and prevented from influencing the assembly. Paul's injunctions were there only for this purpose.

Equally it is good to see the many bible believing churches that have moved to allow women to serve. It would be good for them to recognise the lack of cultural and historical basis in Paul's injunctions. This adjusted view would help in their relationships with the believers who already saw this, but now also need encouragement and help to open the way for full service irrespective of gender. It would help in their existing openness also for the deception possibilities to be recognised, understood and allowed for in terms of ensuring the assembly is protected.

To get here I have highlighted the Greek translation of at least two of the affected passages. This means of course that no previous Discussion on the topic of women in leadership remains relevant, without a serious re-appraisal of these passages.

I have not done an exhaustive study or discussion of all the famous women leaders in the bible. Others before me have done this splendidly. I have tried instead to be exhaustive in what I saw as missing. But I have not been alone. James 1:5 is explicit in this matter:

> If any of you lacks wisdom, let him ask of God, who gives to all liberally and without reproach, and it will be given to him. *James 1:5*

The Lord has taught me much and all credit is His. He is the Teacher. But I have not been alone in another sense too. The enemy has tried to prevent me not just writing this book, but to have me believe false things about women. This perhaps was most apparent when I 'turned'. I remember the place where I was when it dawned on me that the creation order was for the marriage relationship just as the Sabbath was made for man and not man for the Sabbath. On that day I had the very real sensation of a spirit leaving me. Truth had gained the ground necessary for deliverance to be effected from a previously unrealised entity in my life. Of course demonology is a topic foreign to many. It was not to Jesus and as I have explained earlier in this book a matter not to be ignored.

In the early 80s I helped run a church youth group. My experiences of deception up to then had led me to always conclude an evening which involved my teaching from the bible by saying that no one should believe what I had just taught. That is, not until they had read it and seen its validity for themselves in the bible. Paul said similar and indeed we see his practise exampled when he met the Bereans in Acts 17. His words tally with that practise, though here they specifically refer to prophecy I like to use them for all that is presented as material to be believed in:

Test all things; hold fast what is good.   *1 Thessalonians 5:21*

1st Appendix

ANÉR

The aim of this appendix is to show two things. The same word in Greek is used for either a 'husband' or, a 'man'. And secondly whenever it is a 'man', it is always a particular man. So that in plural, it is a particular group of men. It is of note that there is no other Greek word from which to translate the word 'husband'. This is valuable to correctly understand important passages on the issue of women in leadership.

Here follows the word *anér*. There is another Greek word for man commonly used: *anthrópos*. See the separate appendix for *anthrópos*. The reference is first given in the order as found in the New Testament. Then, the word anér in the declension used in the Greek passage. Then the translation in English as found in the NKJV. A few have not been translated in the NKJV and with these I have added in brackets the text in the KJV which shows this appropriately.

It will be readily seen that 'husband' or a (particular) man is always the meaning.

N.B. As mentioned in the preface: notes to the book, I use the letter 'e' with the acute accent 'é' to denote the Greek letter 'eta' (the long 'e') to differentiate from 'epsilon'. Similarly I use the letter 'o' with the acute accent 'ó' to denote the Greek letter 'omega' (the long 'o') to differentiate from 'omicron'.

The declensions of *anér* preceded by those of the definite article (male only)

A declension is the name for the different beginnings and mostly endings of a word to show its relationship with other words in a sentence. The example in English that remains is the genitive case – the name for the relationship of belonging to or, being offspring of. Example: a man's son: where "'s" is the declension of man.

The declensions of the definite article "the" help to identify that the declension for *anér* in the plural nominative is the same as for the plural in the vocative case as found in the New Testament. You may also notice that in highlighting in bold the English translation I also highlight the indefinite article 'a'. There is no separate word in Greek for 'a' and whenever the definite article is not present this is taken by translators from anér itself.

the ho	Nominative	singular	anér	**man/husband**
hoi	(the subject)	plural	andres	
ton	Accusative	singular	andra	
tous	(the direct object)	plural	andras	
tó	Dative	singular	andri	
tois	(the indirect object) for a man/husband – to a man/husband	plural	andrasin	
tou	Genitive	singular	andros	
tón	(the belonging to) of a man/husband – a man's/husband's	plural	andrón	
n/a	Vocative	singular	n/a	
n/a	(the spoken)	plural	andres	

Passages of the New Testament with anér
The Received Text is used throughout

Matthew				
	1:16	ton	andra	Joseph **the husband** of Mary
	1:19	ho	anér	Then Joseph her **husband**
	7:24		andri	**a** wise **man** who built
	7:26		andri	**a** foolish **man** who built
	12:41		Andres	**The men** of Nineveh will rise
	14:21		andres	about five thousand **men**, besides women and children
	14:35	hoi	andres	when **the men** of that place

214

	15:38		andres	four thousand **men**, besides women and children
Mark	6:20		andra	a just and holy **man**
	6:44		andres	about five thousand **men**
	10:2		andri	Is it lawful **for a man** to divorce
	10:12	ton	andra	if a woman divorces her **husband**
Luke	1:27		andri	a virgin betrothed **to a man** whose name
	1:34		andra	since I do not know **a man**
	2:36		andros	had lived with **a husband** seven years
	5:8		anér	for I am **a** sinful **man**
	5:12		anér	behold, **a man** who was full of leprosy
	5:18		andres	behold, **men** brought on a bed . . .
	7:20	hoi	andres	When **the men** had come to Him
	8:27		anér	there met Him **a** certain **man** from the city
	8:38	ho	anér	Now **the man** from whom the demons
	8:41		anér	there came **a man** named Jairus
	9:14		andres	there were about five thousand **men**
	9:30		andres	behold, two **men** talked with Him
	9:32	tous	andras	and **the** two **men** who stood
	9:38		anér	Suddenly **a man** from the multitude
	11:31	tón	andrón	with **the men** of this generation
	11:32		andres	**the men** of Nineveh will rise up
	14:24	tón	andrón	none **of** those **men** who were invited
	16:18		andros	who is divorced from *her* **husband**
	17:12		andres	there met Him ten **men** who were lepers
	19:2		anér	*there was* **a man** named Zacchaeus

	19:7	andri	a guest with **a man** who is a sinner
	22:63 hoi	andres	Now **the men** who held Jesus mocked
	23:50	anér	*there was* **a man** named Joseph, a council member,
	23:50	anér	a good and just **man**
	24:4	andres	behold, two **men** stood by them
John	1:13	andros	nor of the will **of man**, but of God
	1:30	anér	After me comes **a Man** who is preferred before me
	4:16 ton	andra	Go, call your **husband**, and come here
	4:17	andra	I have no **husband**
	4:17	andra	You have well said, 'I have no **husband**'
	4:18	andras	you have had five **husbands**
	4:18	anér	the one whom you now have is not your **husband**
	6:10 hoi	andres	**the men** sat down, in number about five thousand
Acts	1:10	andres	behold, two **men** stood by them
	1:11	andres	**Men** of Galilee, why do you stand
	1:16	andres	**Men** *and* brethren, this Scripture
	1:21 tón	andrón	Therefore, **of** these **men** who have accompanied us
	2:5	andres	Jews, devout **men**, from every nation
	2:14	andres	**Men** of Judea and all who dwell in Jerusalem
	2:22	andres	**Men** of Israel, hear these words
	2:22	andra	Jesus of Nazareth, **a Man** attested by God
	2:29	andres	**Men** *and* brethren, let *me* speak freely
	2:37	andres	**Men** *and* brethren, what shall we do?

3:2		anér	a certain **man** lame from his mother's womb
3:12		andres	**Men** of Israel, why do you marvel
4:4	tón	andrón	the number **of the men** came to be about five thousand
5:1		anér	a certain **man** named Ananias
5:9	ton	andra	those who have buried your **husband** *are* at the door
5:10	ton	andra	buried *her* by her **husband**
5:14		andrón	multitudes **of** both **men** and women
5:25	hoi	andres	Look, **the men** you put in prison
5:35		andres	**Men** of Israel, take heed
5:36		andrón	A number **of men**, about four hundred
6:3		andras	from among you seven **men** of *good* reputation
6:5		andra	Stephen, **a man** full of faith and the Holy Spirit
6:11		andras	they secretly induced **men** to say
7:2		andres	**Men** and brethren and fathers, listen
7:26		andres	**Men**, you are brethren; why do you
8:2		andres	And devout **men** carried Stephen *to his burial*
8:3		andras	and dragging off **men** and women
8:9		anér	there was **a** certain **man** called Simon
8:12		andres	both **men** and women were baptized
8:27		anér	behold, **a man** of Ethiopia, a eunuch
9:2		andras	whether **men** or women
9:7	hoi	andres	And **the men** who journeyed with him

9:12		andra	in a vision he has seen **a man** named Ananias
9:13	tou	andros	I have heard from many about this **man**
9:38		andras	there, they sent two **men** to him
10:1		anér	There was **a certain man** in Caesarea
10:5		andras	Now send **men** to Joppa
10:17	hoi	andres	behold, **the men** who had been sent
10:19		andres	Behold, three **men** are seeking you
10:21	tous	andras	Peter went down to **the men** who had been sent
10:22		anér	*the* centurion, **a just man**, one who fears God
10:28		andri	unlawful it is **for a** Jewish **man** to keep company
10:30		anér	behold, **a man** stood before me
11:3		andras	You went in to uncircumcised **men** and ate
11:11		andres	three **men** stood before the house
11:13		andras	Send **men** to Joppa, and call for Simon
11:20		andres	some of them were **men** from Cyprus
11:24		anér	he was **a good man**, full of the Holy Spirit
13:7		andri	Sergius Paulus, an intelligent **man**
13:15		andres	**Men** *and* brethren, if you have
13:16		andres	**Men** of Israel, and you who fear God
13:21		andra	the son of Kish, **a man** of the tribe
13:22		andra	the *son* of Jesse, *a man after My own heart*
13:26		andres	**Men** *and* brethren, sons of the family of Abraham

13:38		andres	let it be known to you, brethren, that through
			[be it known unto you, **men** *and* brethren, that through KJV]
14:8		anér	in Lystra **a** certain **man** without strength
14:15		andres	**Men**, why are you doing these things?
15:7		andres	**Men** and brethren, you know that a good while
15:13		andres	**Men** *and* brethren, listen to me
15:22		andras	to send chosen **men** of their own company
15:22		andras	and Silas, leading **men** among the brethren
15:25		andras	to send chosen **men** to you
16:9		anér	**A man** of Macedonia stood and pleaded
17:5		andras	some of the evil **men** from the marketplace
17:12		andrón	prominent women as well as **men**
17:22		andres	**Men** of Athens, I perceive
17:31		andri	righteousness by **the Man** whom He has ordained
17:34		andres	However, some **men** joined him and believed
18:24		anér	**an** eloquent **man** *and* mighty in the Scriptures
19:7	hoi	andres	Now **the men** were about twelve in all.
19:25		andres	**Men**, you know that we have our prosperity
19:35		andres	he said: "**Men** of Ephesus, what
19:37	tous	andras	you have brought these **men** here who

20:30		andres	from among yourselves **men** will rise up
21:11	ton	andra	bind **the man** who owns this belt
21:23		andres	We have four **men** who have taken a vow
21:26	tous	andras	Then Paul took **the men**, and the next
21:28		andres	**Men** of Israel, help! This is
21:38		andras	the four thousand assassins [four thousand **men** that were murderers KJV]
22:1		andres	**Men**, brethren, and fathers, hear my
22:3		anér	I am indeed a Jew, born in Tarsus [I am verily **a man** *which am* a Jew KJV]
22:4		andras	delivering into prisons both **men** and women
22:12		anér	Ananias, **a** devout **man** according to the law
23:1		andres	**Men** *and* brethren, I have lived in all good conscience
23:6		andres	**Men** *and* brethren, I am a Pharisee
23:21		andres	**men** who have bound themselves by an oath
23:27	ton	andra	This **man** was seized by the Jews
23:30	ton	andra	the Jews lay in wait for **the man**
24:5	ton	andra	we have found this **man** a plague
25:5	tó	andri	go down with *me* and accuse this **man**
25:14		anér	a certain **man** left a prisoner by Felix
25:17	ton	andra	commanded **the man** to be brought in
25:23	tois	andrasin	**the prominent men** of the city
25:24	hoi	andres	King Agrippa and all **the men** who are here

	27:10	andres	**Men**, I perceive that this voyage will end
	27:21	andres	**Men**, you should have listened to me
	27:25	andres	take heart, **men**, for I believe God
	28:17	andres	**Men** *and* brethren, though I have done nothing
Romans	4:8	anér	*Blessed is **the man** to whom the* LORD
	7:2	tó andri	bound by the law to *her* **husband**
	7:2	ho anér	But if **the husband** dies
	7:2	tou andros	released from the law of *her* **husband**
	7:3	tou andros	if, while *her* **husband** lives
	7:3	andri	she marries another **man**
	7:3	ho anér	but if her **husband** dies
	7:3	andri	though she has married another **man**
	11:4	andras	*for Myself seven thousand men*
1 Corinthians	7:2	ton andra	each woman have her own **husband**
	7:3	ho anér	Let **the husband** render to his wife
	7:3	tó andri	likewise also the wife **to** her **husband**
	7:4	ho anér	her own body, but **the husband**
	7:4	ho anér	likewise **the husband** does not have authority
	7:10	andros	A wife is not to depart from *her* **husband**
	7:11	tó andri	or be reconciled **to** *her* **husband**
	7:11	andra	**a husband** is not to divorce *his* wife
	7:13	andra	a woman who has **a husband**
	7:14	ho anér	**the** unbelieving **husband** is sanctified
	7:14	tó andri	the unbelieving wife is sanctified by **the husband**

	7:16	ton	andra	you will save *your* husband
	7:16		anér	how do you know, O husband, whether
	7:34	tó	andri	how she may please *her* husband
	7:39	ho	anér	as long as her husband lives
	7:39	ho	anér	but if her husband dies
	11:3		andros	the head **of** every **man** is Christ
	11:3	ho	anér	the head of woman *is* **man**
	11:4		anér	Every **man** praying or prophesying
	11:7		anér	**a man** indeed ought not to
	11:7		andros	woman is the glory **of man**
	11:8		anér	For **man** is not from woman
	11:8		andros	but woman from **man**
	11:9		anér	Nor was **man** created for the woman
	11:9	ton	andra	but woman for **the man**
	11:11		anér	neither *is* **man** independent of woman
	11:11		andros	nor woman independent **of man**
	11:12	tou	andros	for as the woman *was* from **the man**
	11:12	ho	anér	so **the man** also *is* through the woman
	11:14		anér	if **a man** has long hair
	13:11		anér	but when I became **a man**
	14:35	tous	andras	let them ask their own **husbands** at home
2 Corinthians	11:2		andri	betrothed you to one **husband**
Galatians	4:27	ton	andra	*Than she who has **a husband***
Ephesians	4:13		andra	to a perfect **man**
	5:22	tois	andrasin	submit to your own **husbands**
	5:23	ho	anér	**the husband** is head of the wife
	5:24	tois	andrasin	to their own **husbands** in everything
	5:25	hoi	andres	**Husbands**, love your wives
	5:28	hoi	andres	So **husbands** ought to love

	5:33	ton	andra	that she respects *her* husband
Colossians	3:18	tois	andrasin	Wives, submit **to** your own **husbands**
	3:19	hoi	andres	**Husbands,** love your wives
1 Timothy	2:8	tous	andras	I desire that **the men** pray
	2:12		andros	to have authority over **a man**
	3:2		andra	**the husband** of one wife
	3:12		andres	be **the husbands** of one wife
	5:9		andros	she has been the wife **of** one **man**
Titus	1:6		anér	**the husband** of one wife
	(2:4		philandrous	the young women to love their husbands)
	2:5	tois	andrasin	obedient **to** their own **husbands**
James	1:8		anér	a double-minded **man**, unstable
	1:12		anér	Blessed *is* **the man** who endures temptation
	1:20		andros	the wrath **of man** does not produce
	1:23		andri	he is like **a man** observing
	2:2		anér	into your assembly **a man** with gold
	3:2		anér	he *is* a perfect **man**, able
1 Peter	3:1	tois	andrasin	submissive **to** your own **husbands**
	3:5	tois	andrasin	being submissive **to** their own **husbands**
	3:7	hoi	andres	Likewise, *you* husbands, dwell with *them*
Revelation	21:2	tó	andri	as a bride adorned **for** her husband

Anér in it's Genitive form *andros*, or *andròn* in the plural

Within the midst of text of Chapter 13 a full breakdown of every verse where *anér* is found in the Genitive singular is given as it is found making use of the simple Genitive (it's basic normal sense). Here I give all the other places where anér is found in the Genitive starting with the basic use as before, but in the plural, then I give all the other uses of the Genitive of *anér* and it's uses in the New Testament.

Andròn this is *anér* in the plural Genitive

. . . 'For I say to you that none **of** those **men** who were invited shall taste my supper.' *Luke 14:24*

Legò - gar - humin, * hoti - oudeis - **tòn** - **andròn** - ekeinòn - tòn - keklémenòn - geusetai - mou - tou - deipnou.

I say - for – to/for you (pl.) * since – no one - **of the** – (of) **men** - those – the [i.e. who] – have been invited – shall taste – of me/my – of the – (of) supper.

* * *

. . . Therefore, **of** these **men** who have accompanied us all the time that the Lord Jesus went in and out among us,
Acts 1:21

Dei - oun - **tòn** - sunelthontòn - hémin - **andròn** - en - panti - chronò - en - hò - eisélthen - kai - exélthen - eph' - hémas - ho - kurios - Iésous,

It is necessary – therefore – **of the** – gathering/consorting – with us – **(of) men** – in – all – time – in – which – he came in – and – he went out – among – us – the – Lord – Jesus,

* * *

However, many of those who heard the word believed; and the number **of the men** came to be about five thousand.
Acts 4:4

Polloi - de - tòn - akousantòn - ton - logon - episteusan, * kai - egenéthé - ho - arismos - **tòn** - **andròn** - hòsei - chiliades - pente.

Many – but – of the – had heard – the – word – they believed,
* and – became/it came to be – the – number – **of the** –
(of) men – about – thousand – five.

* * *

And believers were increasingly added to the Lord, multitudes **of**
both **men** and women,   *Acts 5:14*

. . . mallon - de - prosetithento - pisteuontes - tò - kuriò, *
pléthé - **andròn** - te - kai - gunaikòn.

. . . more – and/but – were added – believers – to the/for the –
(to/for) Lord, * multitudes – **of men** – (both) – and – of women;

* * *

"For some time ago Theudas rose up, claiming to be
somebody. A number **of men**, about four hundred, joined
him. He was slain, and all who obeyed him were scattered and
came to nothing.   *Acts 5:36*

Pro - gar - toutòn - tòn - hémeròn - anesté - THeudas, * legòn
- einai - tina - heauton, * hò - prosekolléthé - arithmos
- **andròn**, * hòsei - tetrakosiòn. * hos - anérethé, * kai - pantes
- hosoi - epeithonto - autò - dieluthésan - kai - egenonto - eis -
ouden.

Before – for – these – the – days – rose up – Theudas, * saying
– to be – someone – himself, * to whom/ for whom – (they)
were joined – a number – **of men**, * about – four hundred; *
who – was put to death, * and – all – as many as – (they)
were persuaded – by him – (they) were dispersed – and – came
– to – nothing.

* * *

> Therefore many of them believed, and also not a few of the Greeks, prominent women as well as **men**.   Acts 17:12

> Polloi - men - oun - ex - autòn - episteusan, * kai - tòn - HEllénidòn - gunaikòn - tòn - euschémonòn - kai - **andròn** - ouk - oligoi.

> Many – (indeed) – therefore – out of/from – them – (they) believed, * and – of the – (of) Greek – (of) women – of the – (of) honourable – and – **of men** – not – a few.

Those were the 6 places where 'of a man' or, 'of a husband' was found in the plural of *anér* as *andròn*. The other use of the Plural Genitive of *anér* (*andròn*) is as follows:

> The queen of the South will rise up in the judgment with **the men** of this generation and condemn them, for she came from the ends of the earth to hear the wisdom of Solomon; and indeed a greater than Solomon *is* here.   Luke 11:31

> Basilissa - notou - egerthésetai - en - té - krisei - meta - **tòn - andròn** - tés - geneas - tautés, * kai - katakrinei - autous. * hoti - hélthen - ek - tòn - peratón - tés - gés - akousai - tén - sophian - Solomòntos, * kai - idou, * pleion - Solomòntos - hòde.

> (A) queen – of [the] south – (she) shall rise up – in – the – judging – with – **the – men** – of the – (of) generation – this, * and – (she) shall condemn – them; * since – she came – out of/from – the – ends – of the – (of) earth – to hear – the – wisdom – of Solomon, * and – look, * (a) more – of Solomon - here.

Here the Genitive is used to denote whether *meta* means 'with' or 'after'. When the word *meta* is followed by the Genitive it means 'with' (plural: *meta tòn andròn* = with the men or, singular: *meta tou andros* = with the man) ; when it is followed by the Accusative it means 'after' (plural: *meta tous andras* = after the men or, singular: *meta ton andra* = after the man). Now follows the other uses of the singular Genitive of *anér* (*andros*):

> Whoever divorces his wife and marries another commits adultery; and whoever marries her who is divorced from *her* **husband** commits adultery.   *Luke 16:18*

> Pas - ho - apoluòn - tén - gunaika - autou - kai - gamòn - heteran - moicheuei. * kai - pas - ho - apolelumenén - apo - **andros** - gamòn - moicheuei.

> Every/All – the (one) – puts away – the – wife – of his – and – marries – (an)other – he commits adultery; * and – all/everyone – the (one) – put away – from – **a husband** – marries – he commits adultery.

Here was the use of the Genetive following the word *apo* which means 'from': *apo an*dros = from a man/a husband. Both the word *ek* = out of/from and *apo* are always followed by the genitive: the ablative or separation use of the Genitive.

> Now there was one, Anna, a prophetess, the daughter of Phanuel, of the tribe of Asher. She was of a great age, and had lived with **a husband** seven years from her virginity . . .   *Luke 2:36*

> Kai - hén - Anna - prophétis, * thugatér - PHanouél, * ek - phulés - Asér. * hauté - probebékuia - en - hémerais - pollais, * zésasa - eté - meta - **andros** - epta - apo - tés - parthenias - autés,

> And – (she) was – Anna – a prophetess, * daughter - (of) Phanuel, * out of/from – tribe – (of) Asher; * she – advanced – in – days – many * (having) lived – years – with – **a husband** – seven – from – the – virginity – of her,

That was as the above last example of the plural given, *meta* followed by the Genitive means 'with'. *Meta andros* = with a husband.

> Then Ananias answered, 'Lord, I have heard from many about this **man**, how much harm he has done to Your saints in Jerusalem.' *Acts 9:13*

> Apekrithé - de - ho - Ananias, * Kurie, * akékoa - apo - pollòn - peri - **tou** - **andros** - toutou, * hosa - kaka - epoiésen - tois - hagiois - sou - en - HIerousalém.

> Answered – but/and – the – Ananias, * Lord, * I have heard – from – many – about – **the** – **man** – this, * how much – evils/'bads' – he did – to the/ for the – (to/for) saints – of You – in – Jerusalem;

Here the Genitive follows the word *peri* and means 'concerning' (i.e. "about such and such . . ."). Followed by the Accusative *peri* means 'approximately' or, '(a-)round'. It is the word from which we obtain periphery or peripheral i.e. around. It refers to a 'circular' thought.

> So then if, **while** *her* **husband** lives, she marries another man, she will be called an adulteress; but if her husband dies, she is free from that law, so that she is no adulteress, though she has married another man. *Romans 7:3*

> Ara - oun - zòntos - **tou** - **andros** - moichalis - chrématisei, * ean - genétai - andri - heterò. * ean - de - apothané - ho - anér, * eleuthera - estin - apo - tou - nomou, * tou - mé - einai - autén - moichalida, * genomenén - andri - eterò.

> So – therefore – living – **while/during which the** – **husband** – (an) adulteress – (she) shall be called, * if – she be – to a man/ for a man – (to/for) another; * if – but – should die – the – husband, * free – she is – from – the – law, * of the

[law] – not – to be – her – an adulteress, * (having) become – to/for a man – another.

The use of the Genitive above is in it's role as 'the time during which'.

For man is not from woman, but woman from **man**.

1 Corinthians 11:8

. . . ou - gar - estin - anér - ek - gunaikos, * alla - guné - ex - **andros**.

. . . not – for – he is – a man – out of/from – a woman, * but – a – woman – out of/from – **a man**;

Here the preposition *ek* is seen. It is always followed by the Genitive. *Ek* means 'out of' or, 'from' (as in 'from the source' as opposed to 'away from').

Nevertheless, neither *is* man independent of woman, nor woman independent of **man**, in the Lord. *1 Corinthians 11:11*

Plén - oute - anér - chòris - gunaikos, * oute - guné - chòris - **andros**, * en - kuriò.

However – neither/nor – a man – apart from – a woman, * nor/neither – a woman – apart from – **a man**, * in – Lord;

This is an example of the preposition *chòris* which means 'apart from'. It is always followed by the Genitive.

2nd Appendix

GUNÉ

Here follows the word *guné*. It is the word from which to translate 'wife' and 'woman'. It is like the French 'femme' since this word is also used for both meanings. The purpose of this appendix is to show the reader that this is indeed interchangeable and thereby it is only the thinking of the translator which determines which is used: either 'wife' or, 'woman'. This is important when it comes to the texts referring to women's roles in church. If the context and immediate passage implies a direct husband connection then the word wife is more appropriate than woman. It is of note that there is no other Greek word from which to translate 'wife'.

The reference is first given in the order as found in the New Testament. Then the word *guné* in the declension used in the Greek passage. Then the translation in English as found in the NKJV.

N.B. As mentioned in the preface: notes to the book, I use the letter 'e' with the acute accent 'é' to denote the Greek letter 'eta' (the long 'e') to differentiate from 'epsilon'. Similarly I use the letter 'o' with the acute accent 'ó' to denote the Greek letter 'omega' (the long 'o') to differentiate from 'omicron'.

The declensions of *guné* preceded by those of the definite article (female only)

A declension is the name for the different beginnings and mostly endings of a word to show its relationship with other words in a sentence. The example in English that remains is the genitive case – the name for the relationship of belonging to or, being offspring of. Example: a woman's son: where " 's" is the declension of woman. You may also notice that in highlighting in bold the English translation I also highlight the indefinite article 'a'. There is no separate word in Greek for 'a' and whenever the definite article is not present this is taken by translators from guné itself.

the	hé	Nominative	singular	guné	**woman/wife**
	hai	(the subject)	plural	gunaikes	
	tén	Accusative	singular	gunaika	
	tas	(the direct object)	plural	gunaikas	
	té	Dative	singular	gunaiki	
	tais	(the indirect object) for a woman/wife – to a woman/wife	plural	gunaixin	
	tés	Genitive	singular	gunaikos	
	tais	(the belonging to) of a woman/wife – a woman's/wife's	plural	gunaikón	
	n/a	Vocative	singular	gunai	
	n/a	(the spoken)	plural	n/a	

Passages of the New Testament with guné
The Received Text is used throughout

Matthew	1:20	tén	gunaika	to take to you Mary your **wife**
	1:24	tén	gunaika	and took to him his **wife**
	5:28		gunaika	whoever looks at **a woman** to lust after her
	5:31	tén	gunaika	*whoever divorces his wife*
	5:32	tén	gunaika	whoever divorces his **wife** for any reason
	9:20		guné	**a woman** who had a flow of blood for twelve years
	9:22	hé	guné	**the woman** was made well from that hour
	11:11		gunaikón	among those born **of women**
	13:33		guné	like leaven, which **a woman** took and hid

232

14:3	tén	gunaika	Herodias, his brother Philip's **wife**
14:21		gunaikón	five thousand men, besides **women** and children
15:22		guné	behold, **a woman** of Canaan came
15:28		gunai	said to her, "O **woman**, great *is* your faith!
15:38		gunaikón	four thousand men, besides **women** and children
18:25	tén	gunaika	sold, with his **wife** and children and all that he had
19:3	tén	gunaika	a man to divorce his **wife** for *just* any reason
19:5	té	gunaiki	*and be joined to his **wife**, and the two*
19:8	tas	gunaikas	permitted you to divorce your **wives**, but from
19:9	tén	gunaika	whoever divorces his **wife**, except for
19:10	tés	gunaikos	the case of the man with *his* **wife**, it is better
19:29		gunaika	or father or mother or **wife** or children or lands
22:24	tén	gunaika	his brother shall marry his **wife** and raise up
22:25	tén	gunaika	no offspring, left his **wife** to his brother.
22:27	hé	guné	last of all **the woman** died also
22:28		guné	in the resurrection, whose **wife** of the seven will she be?
26:7		guné	**a woman** came to Him having an alabaster flask
26:10	té	gunaiki	Why do you trouble **the woman**? For she has done
27:19	hé	guné	on the judgment seat, his **wife** sent to him, saying

	27:55		gunaikes	And many **women** who followed Jesus from Galilee
	28:5	tais	gunaixin	the angel answered and said to **the women**
Mark	5:25		guné	Now **a** certain **woman** had a flow of blood
	5:33	hé	guné	But **the woman**, fearing and trembling, knowing what
	6:17	tén	gunaika	Herodias, his brother Philip's **wife**; for he had
	6:18	tén	gunaika	not lawful for you to have your brother's **wife**
	7:25		guné	For **a woman** whose young daughter had an
	7:26	hé	guné	**The woman** was a Greek, a Syro-Phoenician by birth
	10:2		gunaika	Is it lawful for a man to divorce *his* **wife**?
	10:7	tén	gunaika	*leave his father and mother and be joined to his wife*
	10:11	tén	gunaika	Whoever divorces his **wife** and marries another
	10:12		guné	And if **a woman** divorces her husband
	10:29	hé	gunaika	or brothers or sisters or father or mother or **wife** or children
	12:19		gunaika	brother dies, and leaves *his* **wife** behind, and leaves
	12:20		gunaika	The first took **a wife**; and dying, he left no offspring
	12:22	hé	guné	Last of all **the woman** died also.
	12:23		guné	when they rise, whose **wife** will she be?
	12:23		gunaika	For all seven had her as **wife**.
	14:3		guné	**a woman** came having an alabaster flask

	15:40		gunaikes	There were also **women** looking on from afar
Luke	1:5	hé	guné	His **wife** *was* of the daughters of Aaron.
	1:13	hé	guné	and your **wife** Elizabeth will bear you a son
	1:18	hé	guné	I am an old man, and my **wife** is well advanced
	1:24	hé	guné	after those days his **wife** Elizabeth conceived
	1:28		gunaixin	blessed *are* you among **women**!
	1:42		gunaixin	Blessed *are* you among **women**, and blessed *is*
	2:5		gunaiki	Mary, his betrothed **wife**, who was with child
	3:19	tés	gunaikos	Herodias, his brother Philip's **wife**, and for
	4:26		gunaika	*in the region* of Sidon, to **a woman** who was a widow
	7:28		gunaikón	among those born **of women** there is not a greater
	7:37		guné	behold, **a woman** in the city who was a sinner
	7:39	hé	guné	would know who and what manner of **woman** *this is*
	7:44	tén	gunaika	He turned to **the woman** and said to Simon
	7:44	tén	gunaika	Do you see this **woman**?
	7:50	tén	gunaika	He said to **the woman**, "Your faith has saved you.
	8:2		gunaikes	and certain **women** who had been healed
	8:3		guné	and Joanna **the wife** of Chuza, Herod's steward
	8:43		guné	Now **a woman**, having a flow of blood for twelve years

8:47	hé	guné	Now when the woman saw that she was not hidden
10:38		guné	and a certain woman named Martha welcomed Him
11:27		guné	a certain woman from the crowd raised her voice
13:11		guné	behold, there was a woman who had a spirit of infirmity
13:12		gunai	said to her "Woman, you are loosed from your infirmity."
13:21		guné	like leaven, which a woman took and hid
14:20		gunaika	I have married a wife, and therefore I cannot come
14:26	tén	gunaika	his father and mother, wife and children,
15:8		guné	Or what woman, having ten silver coins, if she
16:18	tén	gunaika	Whoever divorces his wife and marries another
17:32	tés	gunaikos	Remember Lot's wife.
18:29		gunaika	or parents or brothers or wife or children
20:28		gunaika	a man's brother dies, having a wife, and he
20:28	tén	gunaika	his brother should take his wife and raise up
20:29		gunaika	And the first took a wife, and died without children
20:30	tén	gunaika	the second took her as wife, and he died
20:32	hé	guné	Last of all the woman died also.
20:33		guné	in the resurrection, whose wife does she become?
20:33		gunaika	For all seven had her as wife.

	22:57		gunai	saying, "**Woman**, I do not know Him."
	23:27		gunaikón	and **women** who also mourned and lamented Him.
	23:49		gunaikes	and **the women** who followed Him from Galilee
	23:55		gunaikes	And **the women** who had come with Him from Galilee
	24:22		gunaikes	Yes, and certain **women** of our company
	24:24	hai	gunaikes	found *it* just as **the women** had said
John	2:4		gunai	said to her, "**Woman**, what does your concern
	4:7		guné	**A woman** of Samaria came to draw water
	4:9	hé	guné	Then **the woman** of Samaria said to Him
	4:9		gunaikos	ask a drink from me, **a** Samaritan **woman**?
	4:11	hé	guné	**The woman** said to Him, "Sir, You have nothing
	4:15	hé	guné	**The woman** said to Him, "Sir, give me this water
	4:17	hé	guné	**The woman** answered and said, "I have no husband."
	4:19	hé	guné	**The woman** said to Him, "Sir, I perceive that You
	4:21		gunai	Jesus said to her, "**Woman**, believe Me, the hour
	4:25	hé	guné	**The woman** said to Him, "I know that Messiah
	4:27		gunaikos	they marvelled that He talked with **a woman**
	4:28	hé	guné	**The woman** then left her waterpot, went her way

4:39	tés	gunaikos	because of the word **of the woman** who testified
4:42	té	gunaiki	Then they said **to the woman**, "Now we believe
8:3		gunaika	brought to Him **a woman** caught in adultery
8:4	hé	guné	Teacher, this **woman** was caught in adultery
8:9	hé	guné	left alone, and **the woman** standing in the midst
8:10	tés	gunaikos	and saw no one but **the woman**
8:10	hé	guné	He said to her, "**Woman**, where are those accusers
16:21	hé	guné	**A woman**, when she is in labour, has sorrow
19:26		gunai	He said to His mother, "**Woman**, behold your son!"
20:13		gunai	they said to her, "**Woman**, why are you weeping?"

Acts	1:14		gunaixin	supplication, with **the women** and Mary the mother of Jesus
	5:1	té	gunaiki	with Sapphira his **wife**, sold a possession
	5:2	tés	gunaikos	the proceeds, his **wife** also being aware
	5:7	hé	guné	three hours later when his **wife** came in
	5:14		gunaikón	multitudes of both men and **women**
	8:3		gunaikas	and dragging off men and **women**
	8:12		gunaikes	both men and **women** were baptized
	9:2		gunaikas	whether men or **women**, he might

238

	13:50	tas	gunaikas	the devout and prominent **women** and the chief men
	16:1		gunaikos	son of **a** certain Jewish **woman** who believed
	16:13		gunaixin	and spoke to **the women** who met *there*
	16:14		guné	Now **a** certain **woman** named Lydia heard *us*
	17:4		gunaikón	not a few of the leading **women**, joined
	17:12	tón	gunaikón	Greeks, prominent **women** as well as men
	17:34		guné	**a woman** named Damaris, and others with them
	18:2		gunaika	recently come from Italy with his **wife** Priscilla
	21:5		gunaixin	accompanied us, with **wives** and children
	22:4		gunaikas	delivering into prisons both men and **women**
	24:24	té	gunaiki	Felix came with his **wife** Drusilla, who was Jewish
Romans	7:2	hé	guné	For **the woman** who has a husband
1 Corinthians	5:1		gunaika	that a man has his father's **wife**!
	7:1		gunaikos	good for a man not to touch **a woman**
	7:2	tén	gunaika	let each man have his own **wife**
	7:3	té	gunaiki	render to his **wife** the affection due her
	7:3	hé	guné	likewise also **the wife** to her husband
	7:4	hé	guné	**The wife** does not have authority over
	7:4	hé	guné	authority over his own body, but **the wife**

7:10	gunaika	**A wife** is not to depart from *her* husband
7:11	gunaika	a husband is not to divorce *his* **wife**
7:12	gunaika	If any brother has **a wife** who does not believe
7:13	guné	And **a woman** who has a husband who
7:14 té	gunaiki	unbelieving husband is sanctified by **the wife**
7:14 hé	guné	**the** unbelieving **wife** is sanctified by the husband
7:16	gunai	do you know, O **wife**, whether you will
7:16 tén	gunaika	O husband, whether you will save your **wife**
7:27	gunaiki	Are you bound to **a wife**? Do not seek
7:27	gunaikos	Are you loosed from **a wife**? Do not seek
7:27	gunaika	Do not seek **a wife**.
7:29	gunaikas	those who have **wives** should be as though
7:33 té	gunaiki	how he may please *his* **wife**
7:34 hé	guné	There is a difference between **a wife** and a virgin
7:39	guné	**A wife** is bound by law as long as her husband lives
9:5	gunaika	have no right to take along a believing **wife**
11:3	gunaikos	the head **of woman** *is* man
11:5	guné	But every **woman** who prays or prophesies
11:6	guné	For if **a woman** is not covered, let her

240

	11:6	gunaiki	if it shameful **for a woman** to be shorn
	11:7	guné	but **woman** is the glory of man
	11:8	gunaikos	For man is not from **woman**
	11:8	guné	but **woman** from man
	11:9 tén	gunaika	Nor was man created for **the woman**
	11:9	guné	but **woman** for the man
	11:10 hé	guné	For this reason **the woman** ought to have
	11:11	gunaikos	neither *is* man independent **of woman**
	11:11	guné	nor **woman** independent of man
	11:12 hé	guné	For as **the woman** *was* from the man
	11:12 tés	gunaikos	the man also *is* through **the woman**
	11:13	gunaika	Is it proper for **a woman** to pray to God with
	11:15	guné	But if **a woman** has long hair, it is a
	14:34 hai	gunaikes	Let your **women** keep silent in the churches
	14:35	gunaixin	for it shameful **for women** to speak in church
Galatians	4:4	gunaikos	His Son, born **of a woman**, born under the law
Ephesians	5:22 hai	gunaikes	**Wives**, submit to your own husbands
	5:23 tés	gunaikos	the husband is head **of the wife**
	5:24 hai	gunaikes	so *let* **the wives** *be* to their own husbands
	5:25 tas	gunaikas	Husbands, love your **wives**, just as Christ also

	5:28	tas	gunaikas	husbands ought to love their own **wives**
	5:28	tén	gunaika	he who loves his **wife** loves himself
	5:31	tén	gunaika	*be joined to his **wife**, and the two shall*
	5:33	tén	gunaika	so love his own **wife** as himself
	5:33	hé	guné	let **the wife** *see* that she respects *her* husband
Colossians	3:18	hai	gunaikes	**Wives**, submit to your own husbands, as is
	3:19	tas	gunaikas	Husbands, love your **wives** and do not be
1 Timothy	2:9	tas	gunaikas	also, that **the women** adorn themselves
	2:10		gunaixin	which is proper **for women** professing godliness
	2:11		guné	Let **a woman** learn in silence, with all submission
	2:12		gunaiki	And I do not permit **a woman** to teach
	2:14	hé	guné	but **the woman** being deceived, fell into
	3:2		gunaikos	the husband **of** one **wife**, temperate
	3:11		gunaikas	Likewise *their* **wives** *must* be reverent
	3:12		gunaikos	deacons be the husbands **of** one **wife**
	5:9		guné	*unless* she has been **the wife** of one man
(2 timothy	3:6	ta gunaikaria		make captives of gullible women)
Titus	1:6		gunaikos	the husband **of** one **wife**, having faithful children

242

Hebrews	11:35		gunaikes	**Women** received their dead raised to life again
1 Peter	3:1	hai	gunaikes	Likewise *you* **wives** *be* submissive to your own
	3:5	hai	gunaikes	in former times, **the** holy **women**, who trusted in God
	(3:7	tó	gunaikeó	giving honour to the wife)
Revelation	2:20	tén	gunaika	that **woman** Jezebel, who calls herself a prophetess
	9:8		gunaikón	They had hair like **women's** hair, and their teeth
	12:1		guné	**a woman** clothed with the sun, with the moon under
	12:4	tés	gunaikos	the dragon stood before **the woman** who was ready
	12:6	hé	guné	Then **the woman** fled into the wilderness
	12:13	tén	gunaika	he persecuted **the woman** who gave birth
	12:14	té	gunaiki	But **the woman** was given two wings
	12:15	tés	gunaikos	like a flood after **the woman**, that he might
	12:16	té	gunaiki	the earth helped **the woman**, and the earth
	12:17	té	gunaiki	the dragon was enraged with **the woman**
	14:4		gunaikón	not defiled with **women**, for they are virgins
	17:3		gunaika	I saw **a woman** sitting on a scarlet beast
	17:4	hé	guné	**The woman** was arrayed in purple and scarlet
	17:6	tén	gunaika	I saw **the woman**, drunk with the blood of the

243

17:7	tés	gunaikos	the mystery **of the woman** and of the beast
17:9	hé	guné	seven mountains on which **the woman** sits
17:18	hé	guné	And **the woman** whom you saw is that great
19:7	hé	guné	and His **wife** has made herself ready
21:9	tén	gunaika	I will show you the bride, **the** Lamb's **wife**

3rd Appendix

———

ANTHRÓPOS

Here follows the word *anthrópos* in all its forms in the New Testament.

This is useful to help show two things. First that since *anér* is recognised as representing either a particular man or, a husband, *anthrópos* instead is the word which best represents 'someone' or 'a person' and is thus used to denote things referring to men and women in general. So much so that in the plural it is used to refer basically to a group of people which would include women. Examples can be seen below at will, but several are taken and explained in chapter 12.

Second this word which represents the race of man as opposed to a particular man explicitly is often used by Jesus when He called Himself the Son of Man, His favourite title.

The reference is first given in the order as found in the New Testament. Then the word *anthrópos* in the declension used in the Greek passage. Then the translation in English as found in the NKJV.

N.B. As mentioned in the preface: notes to the book, I use the letter 'e' with the acute accent 'é' to denote the Greek letter 'heta' (the long 'e') to differentiate from 'epsilon'. Similarly I use the letter 'o' with the acute accent 'ó' to denote the Greek letter 'omega' (the long 'o') to differentiate from 'omicron'.

The declensions of *anthrópos* preceded by those of the definite article (male only)

A declension is the name for the different beginnings and mostly endings of a word to show its relationship with other words in a sentence. The example in English that remains is the genitive case – the name for the relationship of belonging to or, being offspring of. Example: a man's son: where " 's" is the declension of man.

You may also notice that in highlighting in bold the English translation I also highlight the indefinite article 'a'. There is no separate word in Greek for 'a' and whenever the definite article is not present this is taken by translators from anthrópos itself.

the ho	Nominative	singular	anthrópos	**man**
hoi	(the subject)	plural	anthrópoi	**men/peoples**
ton	Accusative	singular	anthrópon	
tous	(the direct object)	plural	anthrópous	
tó	Dative	singular	anthrópó	
tois	(the indirect object) for a man – to a man	plural	anthrópois	
tou	Genitive	singular	anthrópou	
tón	(the belonging to) of a man – a man's	plural	anthrópón	
n/a	Vocative	singular	anthrópe	
n/a	(the spoken)	plural	n/a	

Passages of the New Testament with anthrópos
The Received Text is used throughout

ho huios tou anthrópou - the Son of Man - literally, "the son of (the) man"

For interest and aesthetics (so it looks good) **tou anthrópou – and Son of Man** have been highlighted. You may notice that 'the' in front of 'Son of Man' is not highlighted in the English whilst 'tou' is in the Greek. This is because the definite article in the English is the translation of 'the Son' and not 'of the Man'. The definite article 'the' thus repeated is not normally translated, but 'dropped'. By this name Jesus called Himself more that any other. It occurs 86 times in the New Testament and was also the name given prophetically of the Lord in the book of Enoch before that. Not such a well known apocryphal book, but is alluded to by Peter and Jesus and directly quoted by Jude:

Now Enoch, the seventh from Adam, prophesied about these men also saying, "Behold, the Lord comes with ten thousands of His saints, to execute judgment on all to convict all, who are ungodly among them of all their ungodly deeds which they have committed in an ungodly way, and of all the harsh things which ungodly sinners have spoken against Him." *Jude 14-15*

Matthew			
	4:4	anthrópos	It is written, '*Man shall not live by bread*
	4:19	anthrópón	I will make you fishers of men
	5:13 tón	anthrópón	thrown out and trampled underfoot by men
	5:16 tón	anthrópón	Let your light so shine before men
	5:19 tous	anthrópous	these commandments, and teaches men so
	6:1 tón	anthrópón	do your charitable deeds before men
	6:2 tón	anthrópón	that they may have glory from men
	6:5 tois	anthrópois	that they may be seen by men
	6:14 tois	anthrópois	For if you forgive men their trespasses
	6:15 tois	anthrópois	But if you do not forgive men their trespasses
	6:16 tois	anthrópois	that they may appear to men to be fasting
	6:18 tois	anthrópois	do not appear to men to be fasting
	7:9	anthrópos	Or what man is there among you
	7:12 hoi	anthrópoi	whatever you want men to do to you
	8:9	anthrópos	For I also am a man under authority

8:20	**tou**	**anthrópou**	but **the Son of Man** has nowhere to lay
8:27	hoi	anthrópoi	And the men marvelled, saying, "Who can this be
9:6	**tou**	**anthrópou**	that you may know **the Son of Man** has power
9:8	tois	anthrópois	who had given such power to men
9:9		anthrópon	He saw a man named Matthew sitting
9:32		anthrópon	they brought to Him a man, mute
10:17	tón	anthrópón	But beware of men, for they will deliver you up
10:23	**tou**	**anthrópou**	the cities of Israel before **the Son of Man** comes
10:32	tón	anthrópón	Therefore whoever confesses Me before men
10:33	tón	anthrópón	But whoever denies Me before men, him
10:35		anthrópon	come to 'set a man against his father
10:36	tou	anthrópou	And 'a man's foes will be those of his own
11:8		anthrópon	go out to see? a man clothed in soft garments
11:19	**tou**	**anthrópou**	**The Son of Man** came eating and drinking
11:19		anthrópos	they say, 'Look, a gluttonous man
12:8	**tou**	**anthrópou**	For **the Son of Man** is Lord even of the Sabbath
12:10		anthrópos	behold, there was a man who had a withered
12:11		anthrópos	What man is there among you who has one sheep

12:12		anthrópos	much more value then is a man than a sheep
12:13	tó	anthrópó	He said to the man, "Stretch out your hand."
12:31	tois	anthrópois	every sin and blasphemy will be forgiven men
12:31	tois	anthrópois	*against* the Spirit will not be forgiven men
12:32	**tou**	**anthrópou**	speaks a word against **the Son of Man**
12:35	ho	anthrópos	A good man out of the good treasure of
12:35	ho	anthrópos	an evil man out of the evil treasure
12:36	hoi	anthrópoi	for every idle word men may
12:40	**tou**	**anthrópou**	so will **the Son of Man** be three days
12:43	tou	anthrópou	unclean spirit goes out of a man
12:45	tou	anthrópou	and the last *state* of that man is worse
13:24		anthrópó	kingdom of heaven is like a man who sowed
13:25	tous	anthrópous	but while men slept, his enemy came
13:31		anthrópos	a mustard seed, which a man took
13:37	**tou**	**anthrópou**	He who sows the good seed is **the Son of Man**
13:41	**tou**	**anthrópou**	**The Son of Man** will send out His angels
13:44		anthrópos	treasure hidden in a field, which a man found
13:45		anthrópó	kingdom of heaven is like a merchant seeking [the kingdom of heaven is like a merchant man, seeking goodly pearls KJV]

13:52		anthrópó	kingdom of heaven is like a householder [the kingdom of heaven is like unto a man *that is* an householder, which bringeth KJV]
15:9		anthrópón	*Teaching as doctrines the commandments of men*
15:11	ton	anthrópon	Not what goes into the mouth defiles a man
15:11	ton	anthrópon	comes out of the mouth, this defiles a man
15:18	ton	anthrópon	come from the heart, and they defile a man
15:20	ton	anthrópon	These are *the things* which defile a man
15:20	ton	anthrópon	unwashed hands does not defile a man
16:13	hoi	anthrópoi	asked His disciples, saying, "Who do men say
16:13	tou	anthrópou	say that I, the Son of Man, am?
16:23	tón	anthrópón	the things of God, but the things of men
16:26		anthrópos	For what is a man profited if he gains the whole
16:26		anthrópos	what will a man give in exchange for his soul
16:27	tou	anthrópou	For the Son of Man will come in the glory of
16:28	tou	anthrópou	taste death till they see the Son of Man coming
17:9	tou	anthrópou	the vision to no one until the Son of Man is risen
17:12	tou	anthrópou	Likewise the Son of Man is also about to suffer

17:14		anthrópos	a man came to Him, kneeling down to Him
17:22	**tou**	**anthrópou**	said to them, "**The Son of Man** is about to be
17:22		anthrópón	betrayed into the hands of men
18:7	tó	anthrópó	woe to that man by whom the offence comes!
18:11	**tou**	**anthrópou**	For **the Son of Man** has come to save
18:12		anthrópó	If a man has a hundred sheep, and one of them
19:3		anthrópó	Is it lawful for a man to divorce his wife
19:5		anthrópos	*For this reason a man shall leave his father*
19:6		anthrópos	God has joined together, let not man separate
19:10	tou	anthrópou	such is the case of the man with *his* wife
19:12	tón	anthrópón	eunuchs who were made eunuchs by men
19:26		anthrópois	said to them, "With men this is impossible
19:28	**tou**	**anthrópou**	in the regeneration, when **the Son of Man** sits
20:1		anthrópó	kingdom of heaven is like a landowner who [the kingdom of heaven is like unto a man *that is* an householder, which went out early KJV]
20:18	**tou**	**anthrópou**	**the Son of Man** will be betrayed to
20:28	**tou**	**anthrópou**	**the Son of Man** did not come to be served

21:25		anthrópón	was it from? From heaven or from men?
21:26		anthrópón	if we say, 'From men,' we fear the multitude
21:28		anthrópos	A man had two sons, and he came to the first
22:11		anthrópon	he saw a man there who did not have
22:16		anthrópón	You do not regard the person of men
23:4	tón	anthrópón	to bear, and lay *them* on men's shoulders
23:5	tois	anthrópois	works they do to be seen by men
23:7	tón	anthrópón	and to be called by men, 'Rabbi, Rabbi.'
(23:14) 23:13	tón	anthrópón	you shut up the kingdom of heaven against men
23:28	tois	anthrópois	outwardly appear righteous to men, but inside
24:27	tou	**anthrópou**	so also will the coming of **the Son of Man** be
24:30	tou	**anthrópou**	the sign of **the Son of Man** will appear in heaven
24:30	tou	**anthrópou**	they will see **the Son of Man** coming on the clouds
24:37	tou	**anthrópou**	so also will the coming of **the Son of Man** be
24:39	tou	**anthrópou**	so also will the coming of **the Son of Man** be
24:44	tou	**anthrópou**	for **the Son of Man** is coming at an hour when
25:13	tou	**anthrópou**	nor the hour in which **the Son of Man** is coming
25:14		anthrópos	like a man travelling to a far country

25:24		anthrópos	I knew you to be a hard man, reaping where
25:31	tou	anthrópou	When **the Son of Man** comes in His glory
26:2	tou	anthrópou	and **the Son of Man** will be delivered up to be
26:24	tou	anthrópou	**The Son of Man** goes as it is written of Him
26:24	tó	anthrópó	woe to that man by whom the
26:24	tou	anthrópou	by whom **the Son of Man** is betrayed!
26:45	tou	anthrópou	at hand, and **the Son of Man** is being betrayed
26:64	tou	anthrópou	hereafter you will see **the Son of Man** sitting
26:72	ton	anthrópon	with an oath, "I do not know the Man!"
26:74	ton	anthrópon	swear, *saying*, "I do not know the Man!"
27:32		anthrópon	they found a man of Cyrene, Simon by name
27:57		anthrópos	there came a rich man from Arimathea

Mark

1:17		anthrópón	make you become fishers of men
1:23		anthrópos	Now there was a man in their synagogue
2:10	tou	anthrópou	that you may know that **the Son of Man** has power
2:27	ton	anthrópon	to them, "The Sabbath was made for man,
2:27	ho	anthrópos	and not man for the Sabbath.
2:28	tou	anthrópou	**the Son of Man** is also Lord of the Sabbath
3:1		anthrópos	and a man was there who had a withered hand

3:3	tó	anthrópó	He said to the man who had the withered hand
3:5	tó	anthrópó	He said to the man, "Stretch out your hand."
3:28	tón	anthrópón	sins will be forgiven the sons of men, and
4:26		anthrópos	as if a man should scatter seed on the ground
5:2		anthrópos	out of the tombs a man with an unclean spirit
5:8	tou	anthrópou	said to him, "Come out of the man, unclean spirit!"
7:7		anthrópón	*Teaching as doctrines the commandments of men*
7:8	tón	anthrópón	you hold the tradition of men – the washing of
7:11		anthrópos	If a man says to his father or mother
7:15	tou	anthrópou	nothing that enters a man from outside
7:15	ton	anthrópon	those are the things that defile a man
7:18	ton	anthrópon	whatever enters a man from outside cannot
7:20	tou	anthrópou	He said, "What comes out of a man,
7:20	ton	anthrópon	that defiles a man."
7:21	tón	anthrópón	from within, out of the heart of men, proceed
7:23	ton	anthrópon	come from within and defile a man
8:24	tous	anthrópous	I see men like trees, walking
8:27	hoi	anthrópoi	saying to them, "Who do men say that I am?"
8:31	**tou**	**anthrópou**	that **the Son of Man** must suffer many

8:33	tón	anthrópón	of the things of God, but the things of men
8:36		anthrópon	what will it profit a man if he gains
8:37		anthrópos	what will a man give in exchange for his soul
8:38	tou	anthrópou	the Son of Man also will be ashamed when He
9:9	tou	anthrópou	till the Son of Man had risen from the dead
9:12	tou	anthrópou	concerning the Son of Man, that He must suffer
9:31	tou	anthrópou	said to them, "The Son of Man is being
9:31		anthrópón	delivered into the hands of men, and they
10:7		anthrópos	*For this reason a man shall leave his father*
10:9		anthrópos	joined together, let no man separate
10:27		anthrópois	Jesus said, "With men *it is* impossible
10:33	tou	anthrópou	and the Son of Man will be delivered to the chief
10:45	tou	anthrópou	even the Son of Man did not come to be served
11:2		anthrópón	a colt tied, on which no one sat [ye shall find a colt tied, whereon never man sat; loose him, and bring *him* KJV]
11:30		anthrópón	was it from heaven or from men? Answer Me
11:32		anthrópón	if we say, 'From men'"- they feared the people
12:1		anthrópos	a man planted a vineyard and set a hedge

12:14		anthrópón	You do not regard the person of men, but teach
13:26	**tou**	**anthrópou**	they will see **the Son of Man** coming in the clouds
13:34		anthrópos	*It is* like a man going to a far country
14:13		anthrópos	Go into the city, and a man will meet you
14:21	**tou**	**anthrópou**	**The Son of Man** indeed goes just as it is written
14:21	tó	anthrópó	of Him, but woe to that man by whom
14:21	**tou**	**anthrópou**	**the Son of Man** is betrayed! It would have
14:21	ho	anthrópos	have been good for that man if he had never
14:41	**tou**	**anthrópou**	behold, **the Son of Man** is being betrayed into
14:62	**tou**	**anthrópou**	you will see **the Son of Man** sitting at the right hand
14:71	ton	anthrópon	I do not know this Man of whom you speak!
15:39	ho	anthrópos	Truly this Man was the Son of God!
Luke 1:25		anthrópois	to take away my reproach among men
2:14		anthrópois	on earth peace, good will toward men!
2:25		anthrópos	behold, there was a man in Jerusalem whose
2:25	ho	anthrópos	name was Simeon, and this man was just
2:52		anthrópois	and stature, and in favour with God and men
4:4	ho	anthrópos	It is written, '*Man shall not live by bread alone*

4:33		anthrópos	in the synagogue there was a man who had a spirit
5:10		anthrópous	From now on you will catch men
5:18		anthrópon	brought on a bed a man who was paralyzed
5:20		anthrópe	He said to him, "Man your sins are forgiven you."
5:24	**tou**	**anthrópou**	you may know that **the Son of Man** has power
6:5	**tou**	**anthrópou**	**The Son of Man** is also Lord of the Sabbath
6:6		anthrópos	And a man was there whose hand was withered
6:8	tó	anthrópó	and said to the man who had the withered hand
6:10	tó	anthrópó	He said to the man, "Stretch out your hand."
6:22	hoi	anthrópoi	Blessed are you when men hate you
6:22	**tou**	**anthrópou**	your name evil, for **the Son of Man**'s sake
6:26	hoi	anthrópoi	Woe to you when all men speak well of you
6:31	hoi	anthrópoi	just as you want men to do to you
6:45	ho	anthrópos	A good man out of the good treasure of his heart
6:45	ho	anthrópos	an evil man out of the evil treasure of his heart
6:48		anthrópó	He is like a man building a house
6:49		anthrópó	like a man who built a house on the earth
7:8		anthrópos	For I also am a man placed under authority

7:25	anthrópon	A man clothed in soft garments?
7:31 tous	anthrópous	To what then shall I liken the men of this generation
7:34 tou	**anthrópou**	**The Son of Man** has come eating and drinking
7:34	anthrópos	and you say, 'Look, a glutton and a wine-bibber [and ye say, Behold a gluttonous man, and a wine-bibber, a friend of publicans and sinners KJV]
8:29 tou	anthrópou	the unclean spirit to come out of the man
8:33 tou	anthrópou	the demons went out of the man and entered the
8:35 ton	anthrópon	came to Jesus, and found the man from whom
9:22 tou	**anthrópou**	**The Son of Man** must suffer many things
9:25	anthrópos	what advantage is it to a man if he gains
9:26 tou	**anthrópou**	of him **the Son of Man** will be ashamed when
9:44 tou	**anthrópou**	for **the Son of Man** is about to be
9:44	anthrópón	delivered into the hands of men
9:56 tou	**anthrópou**	For **the Son of Man** did not come to
9:56	anthrópón	destroy men's lives but to save *them*
9:58 tou	**anthrópou**	**the Son of Man** has nowhere to lay His head
10:30	anthrópos	A certain man went down from Jerusalem to Jericho

11:24	tou	anthrópou	When an unclean spirit goes out of a man
11:26	tou	anthrópou	the last *state* of that man is worse than the first
11:30	**tou**	**anthrópou**	so also **the Son of Man** will be to this generation
11:44	hoi	anthrópoi	and the men who walk over *them* are not aware
11:46	tous	anthrópous	you load men with burdens hard to bear
12:8	tón	anthrópón	whoever confesses Me before men
12:8	**tou**	**anthrópou**	him **the Son of Man** also will confess before
12:9	tón	anthrópón	he who denies Me before men will be denied
12:10	**tou**	**anthrópou**	a word against **the Son of Man**, it will be
12:14		anthrópe	He said to him, "Man, who made Me a judge
12:16		anthrópou	The ground of a certain rich man yielded plentifully
12:36		anthrópois	you yourselves be like men who wait for their master
12:40	**tou**	**anthrópou**	you also be ready, for **the Son of Man** is coming
13:4		anthrópous	worse sinners than all *other* men who dwelt in
13:19		anthrópos	like a mustard seed, which a man took and put
14:2		anthrópos	there was a certain man before Him who had
14:16		anthrópos	A certain man gave a great supper and invited many
14:30	ho	anthrópos	This man began to build and was not able to finish

15:4		anthrópos	What man of you, having a hundred sheep
15:11		anthrópos	He said: "A certain man had two sons.
16:1		anthrópos	There was a certain rich man who had a steward
16:15	tón	anthrópón	justify yourselves before men, but God knows
16:15		anthrópois	what is highly esteemed among men is an
16:19		anthrópos	a certain rich man who was clothed in purple
17:22	tou	anthrópou	one of the days of **the Son of Man**
17:24	tou	anthrópou	so also **the Son of Man** will be in His day
17:26	tou	anthrópou	so it will be also in the days .of **the Son of Man**
17:30	tou	anthrópou	in the day when **the Son of Man** is revealed
18:2		anthrópon	a judge who did not fear God nor regard man
18:4		anthrópon	Though I do not fear God nor regard man
18:8	tou	anthrópou	when **the Son of Man** comes, will he really
18:10		anthrópoi	Two men went up to the temple to pray
18:11	tón	anthrópón	I thank you that I am not like other men
18:27		anthrópois	impossible with men are possible with God
18:31	tou	anthrópou	concerning **the Son of Man** will be accomplished
19:10	tou	anthrópou	**the Son of Man** has come to seek and to save

19:21		anthrópos	I feared you, because you are an austere man
19:22		anthrópos	You knew that I was an austere man
19:30		anthrópón	a colt tied, on which no one has ever sat [ye shall find a colt tied, whereon yet never man sat: loose him KJV]
20:4		anthrópón	was it from heaven or from men?
20:6		anthrópón	if we say, 'From men,' all the people will stone us
20:9		anthrópos	A certain man planted a vineyard, leased it
21:26		anthrópón	men's hearts failing them from fear
21:27	tou	anthrópou	they will see **the Son of Man** coming in a cloud
21:36	tou	anthrópou	and to stand before **the Son of Man**
22:10		anthrópos	entered the city, a man will meet you carrying
22:22	tou	anthrópou	And truly **the Son of Man** goes as it has been
22:22	tó	anthrópó	but woe to that man by whom He is betrayed!
22:48	tou	anthrópou	are you betraying **the Son of Man** with a kiss?
22:58		anthrópe	But Peter said, "Man, I am not!"
22:60		anthrópe	Man, I do not know what you are saying!
22:69	tou	anthrópou	Hereafter **the Son of Man** will sit on the right hand
23:4	tó	anthrópó	I find no fault in this Man

23:6	ho	anthrópos	he asked if the Man were a Galilean
23:14	ton	anthrópon	You have brought this Man to me, as one who
23:14	tó	anthrópó	I have found no fault in this Man concerning
23:47	ho	anthrópos	Certainly this was a righteous Man!
24:7	**tou**	**anthrópou**	**The Son of Man** must be delivered into
24:7		anthrópón	the hands of sinful men, and be crucified

John

1:4	tón	anthrópón	In Him was life, and the life was the light of men
1:6		anthrópos	There was a man sent from God, whose name
1:9		anthrópon	light to every man who comes into the world
1:51	**tou**	**anthrópou**	ascending and descending upon **the Son of Man**
2:10		anthrópos	Every man at the beginning sets out the good wine
2:25	tou	anthrópou	need that anyone should testify of man
2:25	tó	anthrópó	for He knew what was in man
3:1		anthrópos	There was a man of the Pharisees named
3:4		anthrópos	How can a man be born when he is old
3:13	**tou**	**anthrópou**	**the Son of Man** who is in heaven
3:14	**tou**	**anthrópou**	even so must **the Son of Man** be lifted up
3:19	hoi	anthrópoi	and men loved darkness rather than light

3:27		anthrópos	A man can receive nothing unless it has
4:28	tois	anthrópois	went her way into the city, and said to the men
4:29		anthrópon	Come, see a Man who told me all things
4:50	ho	anthrópos	So the man believed the word that Jesus spoke
5:5		anthrópos	Now a certain man was there who had an
5:7		anthrópon	Sir, I have no man to put me into the pool
5:9	ho	anthrópos	And immediately the man was made well
5:12	ho	anthrópos	Who is the Man who said to you, "Take up your
5:15	ho	anthrópos	The man departed and told the Jews
5:27		**anthrópou**	judgment also, because He is **the Son of Man**
5:34		anthrópou	I do not receive testimony from man
5:41		anthrópón	I do not receive honour from men
6:10	tous	anthrópous	Jesus said, "Make the people sit down."
6:14	hoi	anthrópoi	Then those men, when they had seen the sign
6:27	**tou**	**anthrópou**	everlasting life, which **the Son of Man** will give you
6:53	**tou**	**anthrópou**	the flesh of **the Son of Man** and drink
6:62	**tou**	**anthrópou**	if you should see **the Son of Man** ascend where
7:22		anthrópon	and you circumcise a man on the Sabbath

7:23		anthrópos	If a man receives circumcision on the Sabbath
7:23		anthrópon	because I made a man completely well on
7:46		anthrópos	The officers answered, "No man
7:46	ho	anthrópos	ever spoke like this Man!"
7:51	ton	anthrópon	Does our law judge a man before it hears him
8:17		anthrópón	that the testimony of two men is true
8:28	**tou**	**anthrópou**	When you lift up **the Son of Man**, then you will
8:40		anthrópon	seek to kill Me, a Man who has told you the truth
9:1		anthrópon	He saw a man who was blind from birth
9:11		anthrópos	A man called Jesus made clay and anointed
9:16	ho	anthrópos	This Man is not from God, because He does not
9:16		anthrópos	How can a man who is a sinner do such signs
9:24	ton	anthrópon	they again called the man who was blind
9:24	ho	anthrópos	We know that this Man is a sinner
9:30	ho	anthrópos	The man answered and said to them
10:33		anthrópos	You, being a Man, make Yourself God
11:47	ho	anthrópos	For this Man works many signs
11:50		anthrópos	expedient for us that one man should die
12:23	**tou**	**anthrópou**	The hour has come that **the Son of Man** should

12:34	**tou**	**anthrópou**	**The Son of Man** must be lifted up
12:34	**tou**	**anthrópou**	Who is this **Son of Man**?
12:43	tón	anthrópón	loved the praise of men more than the praise
13:31	**tou**	**anthrópou**	Now **the Son of Man** is glorified, and God is
16:21		anthrópos	for joy that a human being has been born
17:6	tois	anthrópois	manifested Your name to the men whom You
18:14		anthrópon	expedient that one man should die for the people
18:17	tou	anthrópou	are not also *one* of this Man's disciples, are you?
18:29	tou	anthrópou	accusation do you bring against this Man?
19:5	ho	anthrópos	said to them, "Behold the Man!"

Acts

4:9		anthrópou	good deed *done* to *the* helpless man
4:12		anthrópois	given among men by which we must be saved
4:13		anthrópoi	they were uneducated and untrained men
4:14	ton	anthrópon	And seeing the man who had been healed
4:16	tois	anthrópois	What shall we do to these men
4:17		anthrópón	they speak to no man in this name
4:22	ho	anthrópos	For the man was over forty years old
5:4		anthrópois	You have not lied to men but to God
5:28	tou	anthrópou	to bring this Man's blood on us

5:29		anthrópois	We ought to obey God rather than men
5:35	tois	anthrópois	you intend to do regarding these men
5:38	tón	anthrópón	keep away from these men and let them alone
5:38		anthrópón	for if this plan or this work is of men
6:13	ho	anthrópos	This man does not cease to speak blasphemous
7:56	**tou**	**anthrópou**	heavens opened and **the Son of Man** standing
9:33		anthrópon	he found a certain man named Aeneas
10:26		anthrópos	stand up; I myself am also a man
10:28		anthrópon	should not call any man common or unclean
12:22		anthrópou	The voice of a god and not of a man
14:11		anthrópois	down to us in the likeness of men
14:15		anthrópoi	We also are men with the same nature
15:17	tón	anthrópón	*that the rest of mankind may seek the LORD*
15:26		anthrópois	men who have risked their lives for the name
16:17	hoi	anthrópoi	These men are the servants of the Most High God
16:20	hoi	anthrópoi	These men, being Jews, exceedingly trouble
16:35	tous	anthrópous	saying, "Let those men go."
17:25		anthrópón	Nor is He worshipped with men's hands

17:26		anthrópón	from one blood every nation of men
17:29		anthrópou	something shaped by art and man's devising
17:30	tois	anthrópois	but now commands all men everywhere
18:13	tous	anthrópous	This *fellow* persuades men to worship God
19:16	ho	anthrópos	Then the man in whom the evil spirit was
19:35		anthrópos	what man is there who does not know that
21:28	ho	anthrópos	This is the man who teaches all *men* everywhere
21:39		anthrópos	But Paul said, "I am a Jew from Tarsus [But Paul said, I am a man *which am* a Jew of Tarsus, *a city* in Cilicia KJV]
22:15		anthrópous	you will be His witness to all men of what
22:25		anthrópon	to scourge a man who is a Roman
22:26	ho	anthrópos	Take care what you do, for this man is a Roman
23:9	tó	anthrópó	We find no evil in this man; but if a spirit or an angel
24:16	tous	anthrópous	a conscience without offense toward God and men
25:16		anthrópon	the Romans to deliver any man to destruction
25:22	tou	anthrópou	I also would like to hear the man myself
26:31	ho	anthrópos	This man is doing nothing worthy of death or chains

	26:32	ho	anthrópos	This man might have been set free if he had not
	28:4	ho	anthrópos	No doubt this man is a murderer, whom, though
Romans	1:18		anthrópón	unrighteousness of men, who suppress the truth
	1:23		anthrópou	an image made like corruptible man
	2:1		anthrópe	you are inexcusable, O man, whoever you are
	2:3		anthrópe	O man, you who judge those practising such
	2:9		anthrópou	on every soul of man who does evil
	2:16	tón	anthrópón	judge the secrets of men by Jesus Christ
	2:29		anthrópón	whose praise *is* not from men but from God
	3:4		anthrópos	let God be true but every man a liar
	3:5		anthrópon	who inflicts wrath? (I speak as a man.)
	3:28		anthrópon	a man is justified by faith apart from
	4:6	tou	anthrópou	the blessedness of the man to whom God imputes
	5:12		anthrópou	through one man sin entered the world
	5:12		anthrópous	thus death spread to all men, because
	5:15	tou	anthrópou	by the grace of the one Man, Jesus Christ
	5:18		anthrópous	came to all men, resulting in condemnation
	5:18		anthrópous	*came* to all men resulting in justification

5:19		anthrópou	For as by one man's disobedience many
6:6		anthrópos	our old man was crucified with *Him*
7:1	tou	anthrópou	the law has dominion over a man as long as he lives
7:22	ton	anthrópon	the law of God according to the inward man
7:24		anthrópos	O wretched man that I am! Who will deliver
9:20		anthrópe	But indeed, O man, who are you to reply against
10:5		anthrópos	*The man who does these things shall live by them*
12:17		anthrópón	regard for good things in the sight of all men
12:18		anthrópón	live peaceably with all men
14:18	tois	anthrópois	acceptable to God and approved by men
14:20.	tó	anthrópó	*it is* evil for the man who eats with offense
1 Corinthians 1:25	tón	anthrópón	foolishness of God is wiser than men
1:25	tón	anthrópón	weakness of God is stronger than men
2:5		anthrópón	in the wisdom of men but in the power of God
2:9		anthrópou	*nor have entered into the heart of man*
2:11		anthrópón	For what man knows the things
2:11	tou	anthrópou	of a man except the spirit
2:11	tou	anthrópou	of the man which is in him?
2:14		anthrópos	But the natural man does not receive
3:3		anthrópon	are you not carnal and behaving like *mere* men?

3:21		anthrópois	Therefore let no one glory in men
4:1		anthrópos	Let a man so consider us, as servants
4:9		anthrópois	apostles, last, as men condemned to
6:18		anthrópos	Every sin that a man does is outside
7:1		anthrópó	*It is* good for a man not to touch
7:7		anthrópous	I wish that all men were even as I myself
7:23		anthrópón	do not become slaves of men
7:26		anthrópó	*it is* good for a man to remain as he is
9:8		anthrópon	I say these things as a *mere* man
11:28		anthrópos	But let a man examine himself, and so let
13:1	tón	anthrópón	I speak with the tongues of men and of angels
14:2		anthrópois	does not speak to men but to God
14:3		anthrópois	edification and exhortation and comfort to men
15:19		anthrópón	we are of all men the most pitiable
15:21		anthrópou	For since by man *came* death
15:21		anthrópou	by Man also *came* the resurrection of the dead
15:32		anthrópon	If, in the manner of men, I have fought
15:39		anthrópón	flesh of men, another flesh of beasts, another of
15:45	ho	anthrópos	*The first man Adam became a living being*

270

	15:47	ho	anthrópos	The first man *was* of the earth, *made* of dust
	15:47	ho	anthrópos	the second Man *is* the Lord from heaven
2 Corinthians	3:2		anthrópón	known and read by all men
	4:2		anthrópón	commending ourselves to every man's conscience
	4:16	ho	anthrópos	Even though our outward man is perishing
	5:11		anthrópous	we persuade men; but we are well known
	8:21		anthrópón	but also in the sight of men
	12:2		anthrópon	I know a man in Christ who fourteen years ago
	12:3	ton	anthrópon	And I know such a man
	12:4		anthrópó	it is not lawful for a man to utter
Galatians	1:1		anthrópón	PAUL, an apostle (not from men
	1:1		anthrópou	nor through man, but through Jesus Christ
	1:10		anthrópous	For do I now persuade men, or God?
	1:10		anthrópois	Or do I seek to please men?
	1:10		anthrópois	For if I still pleased men, I would not
	1:11		anthrópon	preached by me is not according to man
	1:12		anthrópou	For I neither received it from man, nor was I
	2:6		anthrópou	God shows personal favouritism to no man
	2:16		anthrópos	knowing that a man is not justified by the works
	3:12	ho	anthrópos	*The man who does them shall live by them*

	3:15		anthrópon	Brethren, I speak in the manner of men
	3:15		anthrópou	Though *it is* only a man's covenant
	5:3		anthrópó	I testify again to every man who becomes
	6:1		anthrópos	Brethren, if a man is overtaken in any trespass
	6:7		anthrópos	for whatever a man sows, that he will also reap
Ephesians	2:15		anthrópon	create in Himself one new man *from* the two
	3:5	tón	anthrópón	made known to the sons of men
	3:16	ton	anthrópon	through His Spirit in the inner man
	4:8	tois	anthrópois	*And gave gifts to men*
	4:14	tón	anthrópón	by the trickery of men, in the cunning
	4:22	ton	anthrópon	the old man which grows corrupt according to
	4:24	ton	anthrópon	that you put on the new man which was created
	5:31		anthrópos	*For this reason a man shall leave his father*
	6:7		anthrópois	service, as to the Lord, and not to men
Philippians	2:7		anthrópón	*and* coming in the likeness of men
	2:8		anthrópos	being found in appearance as a man
	4:5		anthrópois	Let your gentleness be known to all men
Colossians	1:28		anthrópon	we preach, warning every man
	1:28		anthrópon	and teaching every man in all wisdom

	1:28		anthrópon	that we may present every man perfect
	2:8	tón	anthrópón	according to the traditions of men
	2:22	tón	anthrópón	the commandments and doctrines of men
	3:9	ton	anthrópon	put off the old man with his deeds
	3:23		anthrópois	as to the Lord and not to men
1 Thessalonians	2:4		anthrópois	we speak, not as pleasing to men, but God
	2:6		anthrópón	Nor did we seek glory from men
	2:13		anthrópón	not *as* the word of men, but as it is in truth
	2:15		anthrópois	do not please God and are contrary to all men
	4:8		anthrópon	does not reject man, but God, who has also
2 Thessalonians	2:3	ho	anthrópos	and the man of sin is revealed, the son of
	3:2	tón	anthrópón	from unreasonable and wicked men
1 Timothy	2:1		anthrópón	*and* giving of thanks be made for all men
	2:4		anthrópous	who desires all men to be saved
	2:5		anthrópón	one Mediator between God and men
	2:5		anthrópos	*the* Man Christ Jesus
	4:10		anthrópón	who is *the* Saviour of all men, especially
	5:24		anthrópón	Some men's sins are clearly evident, preceding
	6:5		anthrópón	useless wranglings of men of corrupt minds

	6:9	tous anthrópous	lusts which drown men in destruction
	6:11	anthrópe	But you, O man of God, flee these things
	6:16	anthrópón	unapproachable light, whom no man has seen
2 Timothy	2:2	anthrópois	commit these to faithful men who will be able
	3:2 hoi	anthrópoi	For men will be lovers of themselves
	3:8	anthrópoi	men of corrupt minds, disapproved concerning
	3:13	anthrópoi	But evil men and impostors will grow worse
	3:17 ho	anthrópos	that the man of God may be complete, thoroughly
Titus	1:14	anthrópón	fables and commandments of men who turn from
	2:11	anthrópois	that brings salvation has appeared to all men
	3:2	anthrópous	showing all humility to all men
	3:8 tois	anthrópois	These things are good and profitable to men
	3:10	anthrópon	Reject a divisive man after the first and second
Hebrews	2:6	anthrópos	*What is man that You are mindful of him*
	2:6	anthrópou	*Or the son of man that you take care of him*
	5:1	anthrópón	every high priest taken from among men
	5:1	anthrópón	is appointed for men in things *pertaining* to God
	6:16	anthrópoi	For men indeed swear by the greater, and an oath

	7:8	anthrópoi	Here mortal men receive tithes, but there
	7:28	anthrópous	appoints as high priests men who have weakness
	8:2	anthrópos	which the Lord erected, and not man
	9:27 tois	anthrópois	it is appointed for men to die once, but after
	13:6	anthrópos	*I will not fear. What can man do to me?*
James	1:7 ho	anthrópos	For let not that man suppose that he will
	1:19	anthrópos	let every man be swift to hear, slow to speak
	2:20	anthrópe	do you want to know, O foolish man, that faith
	2:24	anthrópos	You see then that a man is justified by works
	3:8	anthrópón	But no man can tame the tongue
	3:9 tous	anthrópous	and with it we curse men, who have been made
	5:17	anthrópos	Elijah was a man with a nature like ours
1 Peter	1:24	anthrópou	*all the glory of man as the flower of the grass*
	2:4	anthrópón	rejected indeed by men, but chosen by God
	2:15 tón	anthrópón	put to silence the ignorance of foolish men
	3:4	anthrópos	*let it be* the hidden person of the heart, with the [But *let it be* the hidden man of the heart, in that which is not corruptible KJV]

	4:2		anthrópón	for the lusts of men, but for the will of God
	4:6		anthrópous	judged according to men in the flesh, but live
2 Peter	1:21		anthrópou	prophecy never came by the will of man
	1:21		anthrópoi	but holy men of God spoke *as they were* moved
	2:16		anthrópou	a dumb donkey speaking with a man's voice
	3:7	tón	anthrópón	judgment and perdition of ungodly men
1 John	5:9	tón	anthrópón	If we receive the witness of men, the witness of God
Jude	4		anthrópoi	For certain men have crept in unnoticed
Revelation	1:13		**anthrópou**	*One* like **the Son of Man**, clothed with a garment
	4:7		anthrópos	the third living creature had a face like a man
	8:11		anthrópón	and many men died from the water, because
	9:4	tous	anthrópous	but only those men who do not have the seal
	9:5		anthrópon	the torment of a scorpion when it strikes a man
	9:6	hoi	anthrópoi	In those days men will seek death
	9:7		anthrópón	their faces *were* like the faces of men
	9:10	tous	anthrópous	their power *was* to hurt men five months
	9:15	tón	anthrópón	were released to kill a third of mankind
	9:18	tón	anthrópón	a third of mankind was killed- by the fire and the

9:20	tón	anthrópón	But the rest of mankind, who were not killed
11:13		anthrópón	In the earthquake seven thousand men were killed
13:13	tón	anthrópón	from heaven on the earth in the sight of men
13:18		anthrópou	for it is the number of a man: His number is 666
14:4	tón	anthrópón	were redeemed from *among* men, *being* firstfruits
16:2	tous	anthrópous	sore came upon the men who had the mark
16:8	tous	anthrópous	power was given to him to scorch men with fire
16:9	hoi	anthrópoi	And men were scorched with great heat
16:18	hoi	anthrópoi	as had not occurred since men were on the earth
16:21	tous	anthrópous	great hail from heaven fell upon men
16:21	hoi	anthrópoi	And men blasphemed God because of the plague
18:13		anthrópón	and chariots, and bodies and souls of men
21:3	tón	anthrópón	the tabernacle of God *is* with men, and He will dwell
21:17		anthrópou	*according* to the measure of a man, that is,

4th Appendix

AUTHENTEÒ

*A*uthenteò is one of the Greek verbs which occurs in 1 Timothy 2:12. Because this verb is not found elsewhere in the New Testament it requires attention into ascertaining it's meaning. This is especially true since 1 Timothy 2:12 is one of the 3 main texts which has caused much influence on the issue of women in leadership. In the NKJV we find:

> And I do not permit a woman to teach or to have authority
> over a man, but to be in silence.   *1 Timothy 2:12*

Here the verb *authenteò* in it's Infinitive form *authentein* is translated as, 'to have authority'. The next good place to look for the use of a Greek word is the Septuagint since, as a text it was used by the apostles and Jesus: they all quoted directly from it. This is the Greek Version of the Old Testament Hebrew Scripture which was translated about 285-247BC. I expand a little more on this in Chapter 8. However, here also the word was not used. And so the fun begins. The places where it is found are thereby extra-biblical in nature, but the interpretation of it's meaning are heavily dependent on the view of the researcher. This can be seen from the 2 main researches I have read on this matter. The one attributes to *authenteò* an understanding of 'overbearing rule' a 'usurping authority' whilst the other just a plain 'exercise of authority', 'to have authority' (as in the NKJV) without any taste of negative or overbearing pressure.

So, that what I wish to do with this appendix is review these 2 views and thereby end with the most likely of the two's meaning for *authenteò*.

The two researches in question are George W. Knight III's *Authenteò in reference to women in 1 Timothy 2.12* published in *New Testament Studies* Vol. 30 pp. 143–157 and, Catherine C. Kroeger's

Ancient heresies and a strange Greek verb published in *The Reformed Journal* March 1979 pp. 12-15.

Under the fair dealings provisions of the 1988 Copyright Act one may do reviews of works and this is the way in which I intend to use their material.

The interest in Kroeger's work comes from writers for women in leadership. Her conclusions are that the word refers to an overbearing rule. It has a negative emphasis with a sexual overtone. With this understanding it is used to give a picture of a type of authority which Paul advocates women should not use and thereby remove any implication of any other types of 'rule'. However, as I looked and studied her paper I counted about 19 direct sources for the noun similar in form to *authenteò*, but not for the verb itself. Though when I say sources only about 5 were given a place of source reference; the rest were just referred to. As to the verb, Kroeger makes reference to only two direct sources, but again without the means of checking the place of origin: Reference is made to Philodemus and the Byzantine Michael Glycas. There is no other direct source reference to the verb. There are also two indirect sources. To lay so much weight on the meaning of the noun which has a similar form to *authenteò* in order to suggest what the verb means is dependent on how close they are in meaning. This is not automatic since there are verbs which are similar in meaning to the nouns which have a similar look and then there are those with completely different meanings or emphasis. To base the view of one upon the other is possible, but not necessarily accurate methodology. To give examples of this in English: 'to chair' as a verb has to do with directing or overseeing a group of people like in a committee, but 'a chair' as a noun is a piece of furniture you sit on. The meaning of the noun is very different to the verb though the form is similar no matter how many examples you give of the noun it bears no resemblance to the verb in meaning. That is an example at one extreme. Another probably closer to the Kroeger 'formula' is that of the verb 'to need' compared with the adjective 'needy'. I may need advice about something, but no amount of 'needy' emphasising a poor or destitute person will wholly show the truth about the verb 'to need' in the context I gave. And, at the other extreme end of the comparison scale the verb 'to help' is very close in meaning to the noun 'helper'. Suffice to say I have raised enough doubt on Kroeger's work here to show the methodology alone is unhelpful.

Knight's research on the other hand offers not only 10 direct sources for the verb and it's accompanying place of origin so any one can check it out, but of his quotes of Philodemus in *Rhetorica* (1st Century BC) to mean 'those in authority' (they that rule) and Michael Glycas in his *Annals* (12th Century AD) to mean 'to have your own power (authority)' there is clear variance from Kroeger's reading from them. Knight having compared all the 10 sources and used others' translations of these rather than his own so as not to influence the understanding, his conclusion that *authenteò* be placed as a word in the realm of authority, in the objective and neutral sense with the most commonly suggested meaning of 'have authority over' appears to be on somewhat much firmer evidence of a direct kind than anything Kroeger offers. Knight's list of sources came from Bauer, Arndt, Gingrich and Danker's *Greek-English Lexicon of the New Testament and Other Early Christian Literature* plus a few more. These are claimed as more comprehensive and fuller for a meaning source as a whole than offered by Thayer's *Greek-English Lexicon*. He closes by saying the RSV, NAB, NIV and The Translator's Testament have caught the essence of the meaning of *authenteò* and present probably the most satisfactory rendering with their phrase '**to have authority**'.

Of course this meaning or any meaning if not taking into account that the next word is in the Genitive as explained in Chapter Thirteen, profoundly changes the outcome of the use of this alleged meaning. Kroeger's becomes completely ineffective as an argument, whilst Knight's makes full sense if one then looks at what type of authority a husband has been given at the beginning in regards to the one flesh relationship.

LIST OF BIBLE PASSAGES